UP & DOWN

UP &
DOWN

VICTORIES AND STRUGGLES
IN THE COURSE OF LIFE

BUBBA WATSON

WITH DON YAEGER

W Publishing Group

An Imprint of Thomas Nelson

Published in Nashville, Tennessee, by W Publishing Group, an imprint of Thomas Nelson.

Thomas Nelson titles may be purchased in bulk for educational, business, fund-raising, or sales promotional use. For information, please email SpecialMarkets@ThomasNelson.com.

Unless otherwise noted all photos are provided courtesy of Bubba Watson.

Any internet addresses, phone numbers, or company or product information printed in this book are offered as a resource and are not intended in any way to be or to imply an endorsement by Thomas Nelson, nor does Thomas Nelson vouch for the existence, content, or services of these sites, phone numbers, companies, or products beyond the life of this book.

Scripture quotations are taken from the Holy Bible, New International Version®, NIV®. Copyright © 1973, 1978, 1984, 2011 by Biblica, Inc.® Used by permission of Zondervan. All rights reserved worldwide. www. zondervan.com. The "NIV" and "New International Version" are trademarks registered in the United States Patent and Trademark Office by Biblica, Inc.®

Library of Congress Control Number: 2021943310
ISBN 978-0-7852-9201-2 (HC)
ISBN 978-0-7852-9203-6 (eBook)
ISBN 978-0-7852-9204-3 (audio)

Printed in the United States of America

21 22 23 24 25 LSC 10 9 8 7 6 5 4 3 2 1

To my wife, Angie, the love of my life. Your support has helped me grow into a better man. Nothing in this world means more to me than being your husband.

To Caleb and Dakota, you are the most amazing gifts I could have ever received. I will cherish you always.

—Bubba Watson

To Jeanette, thanks for navigating life's ups and downs with me and making projects like this possible!

—Don Yaeger

To be yourself in a world that is constantly trying to make you something else is the greatest accomplishment.

RALPH WALDO EMERSON

CONTENTS

AUTHOR'S NOTE

This is not a typical golf book. I had the chance to write a typical golf book a few years ago after I'd won my second Masters Tournament. The cover was going to be jet black with my name written in bright pink. That book would have told the life story of "golfer Bubba Watson" at the height of fame and laid out my accomplishments for all to see, with carefully crafted nods of thanks to this person and that person. Ultimately, I decided not to do the project. I knew the picture of "success" everyone expected that book to portray would not have been the truth. Well, it would have been true, but it would have been only half of the story because I was not personally ready to reveal the whole story back then. Thank God I waited.

If we had done it, you'd have missed my ups and downs: my growth as a husband, father, son, friend, Christian, businessman, and, yes, underwear model. (Okay, I had to put that last one in there.) If I'd done the book then, you'd have missed the opportunity to grow along with me through a deeper, more complicated, and hopefully relatable story, a story that I'm undertaking to tell in this book, right now.

If you love the game of golf or follow me as a fan, I hope that my writing a book that isn't a pure golf book won't turn you away. I'm writing this as much for you as for anybody else. You don't honestly think I could write about myself and not include a healthy dose of golf in it, do you?

But I had no interest whatsoever in writing out my life story as an unfolding series of nice, neat chapters that chronicled all my wonderful accomplishments. The truth is, as with most people, my life has been anything but nice and neat. More often than not, it has consisted of ups and downs, triumphs and humiliations, moments of joy, mistakes, and misunderstandings that I've had to struggle with and learn from, thanks to some very dear people in my life. Everybody battles with their own personal set of demons, and if you know anything at all about me, you know I've battled plenty of them as well. The difference between most people and me, I suppose, is that most folks don't do all the good and bad things in front of millions of people.

In a way this book tells the story of the challenges I wrestled with my whole life, the people I love who stuck by me even when it felt like I didn't deserve their loyalty, and the life I'm still very much in the process of building. It's also a record of how, through my marriage to Angie, I drew closer to Jesus Christ and asked him to help me apply the Bible's teachings to everything I do.

It's an attempt to bring together the public perception of me as the small-town Bubba from Bagdad with my struggle to express my true self and feel like I belong. For example, you may like me because I play with a pink driver or because I enter-tain you on social media (#UrWelcome for those in the know). You may like me because I've adopted kids and become, along with Angie, something of a spokesperson for the positive ways in which adoption can change young lives. Or you may not care for me very much because you've seen or read about me blowing up on a course and yelling at my caddie or a spectator. For better or worse, I am all of these things and none of them at the same time.

I know it's not pretty when somebody loses their composure in heated moments, but imagine how it feels watching your own bad moments get replayed over and over on ESPN, knowing you can never really take it back, no matter your level of regret.

It seems, well, unsportsmanlike.

What I hope you'll take away from spending some time with me in this book is that I am a man working to be better tomorrow than I am today. I hope you'll connect with me through this and realize, with a laugh or twenty along the way, that we're more alike than different. Golf happens to be what I do. It's not who I am. So, who is this character named Bubba Watson? Well, you're going to have to read the book to find that out.

———

Suffice to say, I grew up in a household and an era when men were supposed to be stoic and self-sufficient, to let their actions speak for themselves. Sometimes this code of behavior has worked well for me. It helped me achieve a near superhuman focus on developing my gifts with a golfclub to the point where I became known as a child prodigy who shot 62 for eighteen holes at the age of twelve; who won a couple of Masters tournaments and soared to number two in the world; and who earned the opportunity to compete for his country in the Ryder and Presidents Cups and even the Olympics. No one grows up believing these things are possible, much less a kid from Bagdad, Florida, population 3,800.

I've tried to appreciate each and every one of the amazing opportunities that a life playing golf has given me. But even with that appreciation, the truth is that every dream has two sides.

When I hit the hook shot out of the woods to help me win the 2012 Masters, I had no idea how it would impact my life. Sure, I had always dreamed of being a Masters champion, but as I said in the post-round interview, that is where the dream stopped. I never thought about what would happen after the last putt dropped, but I quickly realized I was not equipped mentally or emotionally for living my dream in the public eye. I'm not particularly proud of this fact, but it's the truth. I'm a guy who found something he was good at early in life, then pursued it relentlessly with blind faith and no backup plan. When I started having some level of success on the course, I let that go to my head. I am painfully aware that at times I was difficult to be around, and eventually that rightfully earned me a long spell of public distaste—and even rejection.

In this book, I'll look at the influences of my family life as well as the decisions I made early on about golf that helped shape me as an adult. Many folks think that professional athletes (and celebrities in general) live in a perpetual bubble, shielded from the public's perceptions of them, but I'm living proof that this is not always the case. I care a lot about what the public thinks of me. I want to be liked by people, not because I want to be best friends with everyone in the world or anything like that, but I do want my contribution to the world to be one of joy, not division or rancor.

Some people want their public figures to be perfect so they can lose themselves in a fantasy about living a charmed life; other people want to see them dragged through the dirt in order to make them feel better about their own lives. Neither of those types of reader will find exactly what they're looking for in these pages. But, if you see a little piece of yourself or your loved ones in my ups and downs, then this book is for you.

You know the kinds of ups and downs I'm talking about: trying to be a great dad and a great husband, trying to find the time and commitment to have a successful career. Trying to deal with pressure and anxiety, both from others and self-imposed. On this last score, successful professional golfers tend to fall into one of two buckets.

The first group are those with strong, disciplined minds who are able to compartmentalize everything in their lives—from quickly forgetting the pressure they've heaped on themselves from a single bad shot on a given hole, to letting go of the frustration of seeing false stories about them in the media. Frankly, I'm in awe of these folks.

The second group are those who are less disciplined in their minds but learn to disguise their emotions and vulnerabilities so they at least look like the first group. I fall into this category and spent too many years trying to bury the truth. For years I thought the best way to deal with pressure was to internalize it and for the most part deny its existence. As you'll learn in this book, that approach led to a total physical and emotional breakdown that made me fear for my life. But the truth is, I never had a prayer of hiding my struggles. Not by a long shot.

My dad told me the only thing a poor man has in this world is his word. So never lie. I don't care how bad the truth is. Never lie. I'm not a poor man, but I am proud to say this book was written in the same spirit. I will never know for sure, but I hope the old soldier would be proud.

CHAPTER 1

Rock Bottom

I can see it in the mirror. Everyone can see it. I am standing on a scale a lot these days: watching the pounds fall off as I become rail thin. I'm too weak to hit many of the shots that led me to two green jackets in three years. It's the spring of 2017 and I'm on my bathroom scale in our home in Pensacola. My feet tremble as *162* comes across the digital screen.

162.

The number doesn't flash at me; it screams.

In a fog, I move from the bathroom into the bedroom. I fall to my knees and cry out to the Lord. *I don't know what you want me to do,* I say. *I don't know what to do. Help me. Help me!*

I was at a breaking point. I had been losing weight for nearly a year. A decade ago, I had been pushing 210 pounds. I had slimmed down twenty pounds by giving up everything that tasted good—cheeseburgers, chocolate cake, and sodas. At 190 pounds, I had the energy and power to compete at the top of the game. When I saw 162 on the scale, I thought I was dying. There was something going on in my body that no one could find. Three or four doctors had looked at me with blood tests and heart monitors. "Bubba, there is nothing wrong with you," they told me. "It looks like you eat fish every day."

But I'm a fearful guy. The Bible teaches us to not fear death, but I was worried that this was the end of my life. I thought back to 2010 when I watched my father, Gerry, go through throat cancer and wither away from 190 pounds to 92 pounds in less than a year. I remembered bathing him three days before he passed away. You never dream of bathing a grown man, especially your father. So here I was losing weight and wondering if I had throat cancer or some other terminal disease and getting ready to die and leave my family.

On the golf course and off it, my mind tended to go quickly from one extreme to another. I could have a 5-under round going and then have a single bad break with my ball settling into a divot and feel like everything was falling apart. The difference was that on the golf course I could make a birdie that would turn my mood from bad to good, but when it came to my weight there was no way for a quick rebound that could help settle my mind. When I started losing weight my first instinct was that I was dying. And the more anxiety I had around thoughts of death, the more fearful I became and the less I was capable of coping with the stress.

One of my biggest downfalls is that my mind races, but my mind also is such a beautiful thing that's helped me tremendously as I've worked to become a great golfer. It's my mind that in 2012 conceived hooking a modern golf ball 40 yards with a 52-degree wedge out of the woods to 10 feet at Augusta National to win my first Masters in a playoff. But my mind is also tremendously stubborn and now its stubborn will was threatening everything that I had worked for. Something had to give. That's when I fell on my knees and begged God for help.

I didn't grow up in the church. I didn't learn as a child how to say prayers before I went to bed or before meals. When I was nineteen years old, I went to a church service for the first time with a neighbor, but it wasn't until I met my wife, Angie, at the University of Georgia that I began seriously to commit myself to Christ. Shortly after we were married in 2004, Angie and I were baptized together the day after Christmas. I can't say I knew I was going to have that moment when I saw 162 on my bathroom scale. Perhaps it's like in golf when you finally see an instructor to correct flaws after years of frustrating play. I don't know much about that, having preferred to figure things out on my own for most of my career, but I understood that my mind, and my fears, were problems I couldn't solve without God.

Very few people in the world of golf knew the ordeal that I was facing with my weight, and how I had let the pressure to succeed in the game while trying to be a good husband, father, and friend drive me to the lowest place in my life. Teddy Scott, who as my caddie was around me more than anyone, didn't know that I was worried about my weight. He could see that I was losing weight, but like most others he didn't see it as a huge problem. In some ways, having so many people telling me that I looked good when I felt like crap seemed to make me feel worse. Not that anyone meant harm. After all, no one really knew what was going on because I was hiding it from all but a few people.

Mostly what Teddy and others did notice during this period was how I lost my confidence as a golfer. I was a master of deflecting my pain, cracking jokes during matches and cutting rap songs with other golfers, which I'll tell you about later. I projected an image of good health. I didn't know how to ask for help. I wasn't taught to ask for help. On the golf course, I started eating energy-boosting protein balls made of organic oats, ground flaxseed, peanut butter, and chocolate protein powder. But I kept losing too much weight. I had excruciating pain in my stomach when I felt pressure or anxiety. Golf was killing me. I was letting my position on the money list, world rankings, and Ryder Cup and Presidents Cup standings eat at my soul. And as I changed my diet to try to handle the pains caused by the stress, I began to lose more weight and energy because I simply was not eating enough to provide my body with the nutrition it needed.

Ultimately, I accepted that it was my mind and not my body that was causing the stress, anxiety, pain, and weight loss. I wouldn't go so far as to say I was depressed. I never thought about it that way. It was just an out-of-control mind, racing with fear and anxiety. I contemplated retirement. I told myself that if I retired from golf, I could live my life beautifully and not have these stresses.

"I need to be here for you and the kids," I told Angie. "I will quit golf if it is causing me all this stress and making me slowly wither away to death."

"But you love golf," she said. "Why would you do this? It's a mind thing. It's not a three-putt on the golf course that's causing this. If you quit golf your mind is going to go to something else."

I was letting the whole world dictate how I felt because I wanted to please everyone. I don't like seeing negatives about me and couldn't let them go. I had grown up my whole life being negative and talking negative. The negativity had to do with my fear of disappointing people. To change that outlook, I was told to see a psychologist or mental coach, but I said no. I thought I could do it myself.

A year before my weight sunk to 162 pounds, my life had

begun spiraling in the wrong direction. My main priorities in 2016 had been to make the Ryder Cup and Rio Olympic teams. Rio was particularly a huge deal considering it was the first time golf had been staged at the Olympics since 1904. I was consumed by the thought of failing one of the drug tests administered by the PGA Tour and International Olympics Committee. Even though I had never taken illegal drugs or been drunk or taken much more than Advil, I was worried that I would get a false positive on a drug test and they would take my career away from me. This may seem irrational but that's how I felt.

I would qualify for Rio, where I finished in a tie for eighth. Teddy didn't make the trip for personal reasons, but he texted me Bible verses and his viewpoints on the course set-up. Randall Wells, my business partner and childhood friend, stepped in to caddie. The whole experience of being an Olympian is very different from being just a golfer. I got to meet Greg Louganis, the four-time Olympic gold medalist diver, and athletes from several different sports. It definitely brought some perspective to my life as a professional golfer. Most of the Olympic athletes had trained for years to peak during these two weeks. Many of them only got one shot at the biggest event of their life, since the Olympics are only held every four years. As a golfer, I consider the Masters to be my biggest event, and I get to play it every year.

After failing to secure an automatic qualifying spot on the 2016 Ryder Cup team, I was left needing a captain's pick to get a spot on the team. When Ryan Moore ended up getting the last captain's pick, it hit me pretty hard. Ryan deserved to be picked over me for the last spot on the Ryder Cup team, because he had finished in the top ten in all four playoff events. Yet I was still hurt and embarrassed after being left off the team. In most years, being ranked ninth in the team standings and seventh in the world ranking would have pretty much assured me a spot on the team. When I got the news from captain Davis Love III, I asked him to let me join him as a vice-captain, which he accepted. Still, negative thoughts dominated my head. *Do people hate me? Do they not think I'm good enough to play on a team? Do people not want to partner with me? Why do I have to be a vice-captain?*

The effects of that stressful period carried over into 2017 as I continued to lose weight. During the offseason I switched to a Volvik colored golf ball after playing a Titleist for most of my career. With a pink ball, I was going to grow the game in a different way. When I was growing up, I used a two-toned PING ball, so the idea of playing a colored ball certainly felt nostalgic. Because Volvik wasn't a widely played brand on the PGA Tour, a lot of people questioned my decision to change balls after having so much success with the Titleist Pro V1x. No one seemed to care how much research or testing I had done before making the switch. The feeling that everyone was second-guessing the change did impact me mentally. Having finished the prior year poorly, the extra mental stress made it even harder for me to rebound in 2017. I let my mind take me out of where I wanted to be. Every time I hit a bad shot, I started to believe that I wasn't good enough, and perhaps would never be good enough again.

"It's your mind," my caddie, Teddy Scott, told me. "You're not having fun with golf. You're letting all this other stuff in your life dictate how you feel. You need to relax."

That year I missed the cut at three of the four majors and was knocked out of the FedEx Cup playoffs after two events. At the 2017 Masters I thought I played great, but I missed the cut there for the first time in nine appearances. Teddy and I compared all the data from 2017 to previous years and found that my loss of power was changing the way I played Augusta National. I simply wasn't swinging the club with as much power or speed as I had in the past, before I started losing weight. I started drinking high-calorie smoothies a couple of times a day to gain weight.

In my conversations with the Lord, I admitted to him that I didn't know if it was dumb to change equipment in the middle of my physical and mental struggles. While my concern had not yet peaked, I already knew I was losing too much weight. I knew something was wrong but couldn't really accept it at the time. I required medication for air travel because every time I got on an airplane, I thought I was going to have a heart attack. Everybody from my doctor to my wife to my caddie was telling me that I just needed to change my mindset.

Why was I so fearful if I trusted what I read in the Bible? I had a beautiful wife who loved me unconditionally. We had two beautiful kids and we were giving them the best life we could possibly give them. I had achieved my golf dream of winning the Masters not once, but twice. So what was I truly fearing and why was I letting this negativity get to me? I was trying to fight through this. I didn't want to sit at home. I was going to fight through it on the golf course. I got stronger and deeper into the Word of God. I began a new prayer: *Lord, if you're going to take me, I want you to take me. But I want to live every day being the best husband and the best dad that I can be. I love the game of golf and I believe that you gave me the talent to play it. So just let me enjoy the moments that I have left here on this earth.*

I don't remember the scripture that came up on my Bible app when I was down on my knees in the bedroom, but I know it was positive and it helped me grow closer in my relationship with God. The Bible is my book of positivity that I have to go to daily or my mind is going to run the opposite direction to a very dark place.

I cry easily. I cry during church. At my wedding I battled tears so long the small crowd in attendance began to wonder if I was going to get through my vows. I cried in 2005 when I finished twenty-first on the Nationwide Tour (now called the Korn Ferry Tour), the last spot to earn a PGA Tour card. I cried in 2010 at the Travelers Championship in Hartford when I won for the first time on tour. In 2014 I cried after winning my second Masters in three years when I saw my two-year-old son, Caleb, approaching me as I walked off the eighteenth green. But I doubt if I have ever had a cry more beneficial to my life than the one I had when I was on my knees, steps from my bathroom, with what I believed was my future hinging on the numbers on the scale.

These tears, and my faith, ultimately saved my life.

CHAPTER 2

62 & the Start of an Obsession

I remember the day when I became Bubba Watson the golfer and not just a kid wearing knickers trying to emulate Payne Stewart, my favorite player. I was thirteen years old and it was the last round of the 1992 Divot Derby, the biggest junior golf tournament in the Pensacola area. I shot 71 in both the first and second rounds to take a commanding lead into the last day at Tanglewood Golf Club, my home course. Seven years earlier I had one club, a cut down, left-handed 9-iron that allowed me to learn the game. I spent hours hitting plastic balls around our house in Bagdad—around trees, under trees, and over the house. I had been playing the Derby—and winning my age division— every year since I was eight years old. But on this day, I was going to make a splash that everyone was going to notice.

I knew with such a big lead heading into that third day that I couldn't lose the tournament unless I failed to complete the round. At Tanglewood, a public course in Milton that some play-fully called "Tangleweed" because of its modest conditioning, we played the red tees and there were three or four holes with temporary greens, which made the course play even shorter.

Eleven-hundred yards longer from the back tees, where I usually played, my lowest score was 70. For the Divot Derby some of the holes were drivable and at one point in the round I reeled off six birdies in a row.

As I was walking down the twelfth fairway, I heard a familiar voice shout out, "How you playing?" It was Boo Weekley, whose family lived on the course.

"Good," I answered.

"He hasn't made any bogeys," said my dad, who was following our group in a golf cart.

Boo Weekley was asking about *my* round. I looked up to him and Heath Slocum. Five years older than me, they were my role models. It wasn't like it is today with 24-7 coverage of all sports stars on ESPN, Golf Channel, and social media. Heath and Boo were the two people I saw every day after school at the golf course. They each were already multiple winners in the Divot Derby and the best players in town. It was a dream world whenever I got to play with them. They were going to college and would one day make the PGA Tour. Everyone in town was sure of it.

I wasn't done with my round but the encounter with Boo made me feel like a champion already. I would up end shooting a bogey-free, 10-under-par 62, with ten birdies for a 46-shot victory. Later after the round I ran into Boo again in the clubhouse.

"What did you shoot?" he asked.

"Sixty-two," I said.

"What!" he said.

I didn't know whether to take Boo's gesture as genuine amazement or shock that I had shot 62. I had not given him or anyone else much reason to believe that I could play that level of golf. I was good for my age, but I hadn't shot 62! But on that day

I did and suddenly I felt different. I got comfortable with the idea that golf was in my future.

People told me that I was never going to be as good as Heath, whom everyone thought was the most likely of the three of us to do something special. In high school, Boo was a good player but had a reputation for not taking the game all that seriously. By his own admission, he was more interested in fishing and hunting than he was golf. Yet when he came back after a year of junior college, he was a phenomenal player. Among the golfing crowd in town, there were lots of opinions about who between the three of us might become regulars on the Tour. I don't think anybody thought that all three of us would make it.

When people were choosing who they thought would make the Tour, I was an unconventional choice. I was a left-hander who played the game very differently than most thought I should. I didn't always play the odds. To some, I was hard-headed and flamboyant, too brash to make safe choices on the golf course. My parents would allow and even encourage me to do things differently simply for the sake of having my own way or to stand out from the rest of the kids. My dad had reached out to a PGA Tour golfer who lived nearby, Joe Durant, for advice on how to guide my development. Joe is a four-time PGA Tour winner who had come up through mini tours and had actually won the same Divot Derby years earlier. My dad knew Joe because he had been the best man at Joe's brother's wedding. After watching me hit a few shots, Joe told my dad that he thought I had a gift and that the last thing I needed was somebody trying to tell me how to play.

Growing up at Tanglewood, I played nearly every day with my best friend, Randall Wells, who lived across the street from the course. His parents bought their house from Hiram Cook, the left-handed club pro who gave me that 9-iron. When my dad played with his friends, I would swat balls with it as I trailed his golf cart. Dad would have me aim at signs located in the fairways. After a couple of times of hitting the target, my dad would say, "That would have been a good shot if you had aimed at a real target" (like the green, or hole). It became an inside joke with me, my dad, and my mom, who caddied for me, about my development in the game.

I don't know if there are any kids who played as much as Randall and me. In the summers my dad would drop me off in the morning before he went to work and pick me up on the way home at Randall's house, often after dark. Because of the way the fog lights beamed on his Eagle Talon, we could always tell it was my dad driving down the main road in front of the course. Dad often would find us shooting basketball in Randall's driveway. Sometimes my dad would park and let me practice in the dark under a dingy, orange-tinted light pole over the practice putting green. While I worked on my putting and chipping, he would have a cigarette and a beer. My mom and my sister would come out too. Dad was the closest thing that I ever had to a teacher. Yet his instruction was more homespun wisdom than anything technical. "Swing hard," he would say, "in case you hit it, and we'll figure it out later."

In 1991, Payne Stewart won the US Open at Hazeltine in an 18-hole playoff over Scott Simpson. I watched every shot and imagined what it would be like to play on the Tour. That summer on the putting green in contests with Randall at Tanglewood, I tried to put myself in a frame of mind to win a major champion-ship. *This 10-foot putt is to win the Masters. This 30-footer will get me into a playoff at the US Open.* I use a lob wedge now almost exclusively around the greens because of how I learned to use it at that putting green. Randall and I made up holes chipping to the putting green from every conceivable spot; we would start on the first tee box or the flower bed next to the clubhouse. The crazier the made-up hole seemed, the better. We let our imaginations run wild. I spent countless hours playing our little made-up holes.

I've often said that the straight shot is the hardest one for me to hit, and I don't like to hit it straight very often. I've become known for my ability to curve the ball both left to right and right to left in some pretty spectacular ways. Thirty years ago, curving the ball didn't seem like that big a thing, but my game gets more attention now because golf ball technology, with advanced dimple patterns and reduced spin rates, forces the ball to fly straighter than it did thirty years ago. When I first learned the game in the 1980s, the best players used a Balata golf ball, a soft wound ball that was easier to spin and curve in the air. I see shapes on the golf course because I learned to play with those Balata balls and because of the course I grew up playing. Tanglewood has a lot of doglegs, holes that curve. It also provides a lot of opportunity to curve the ball because there is very little grass outside the tree-lined fairways. When you hit it in the trees you are often playing from hard compact dirt or pine straw, which allows a player to make clean contact and put a lot of side spin on recovery shots. Spin is the key to making the ball curve and a part of the game that fascinates me. If I had grown up on a golf course with a bunch of straight holes and thick, high rough, I would not have been able to express my creativity and I might not have fallen in love with the game. I probably would not have made it to the PGA Tour, and I definitely wouldn't have the shots that I have today. I knew that I could hit that 40-yard hook off the pine straw in the playoff at the 2012 Masters because I have had to hit shots like that on nearly every hole at Tanglewood. Some golf courses would never give you a chance to practice that shot.

A few years ago, I took my caddie, Teddy Scott, out to Tanglewood so that he could see how I developed my game. Teddy is a good player. He played the mini tours before he turned to caddying. At Tanglewood we played in a little recurring money game organized by a group I had played with many times, and I picked him to be on my team. I had him hit irons off the tee on many holes to keep something in play while I hit my driver on nearly every hole. Because of my length I can't really play most of the Tanglewood's doglegs as they are designed. So I got very comfortable over the years hitting the ball over trees, cutting out the dogleg altogether with high booming shots. People who didn't know where I was hitting it would think I was aiming for somebody's backyard on purpose. On one particular dogleg right, I had Teddy hit a 3-iron to the corner of the dogleg. I took my driver and aimed right and hit a towering shot over a house with a 50-yard slice. I knew it was perfect. When we got up to the green, I was ten feet off the back edge. Teddy was amazed by the shot, but he knew better than most that I love being creative on the course.

———————

Bagdad is a tiny mill town sandwiched between two bodies of water, the Blackwater River and Pond Creek, in Santa Rosa County, twenty miles from Pensacola. Its namesake, the more famous one in Iraq, also sits between two bodies of water— the Tigris and Euphrates Rivers. The two cities had the same spelling until the British added an *h* to the spelling of the Iraq city. For years, Bagdad was a lumber town, but once the military installations began flooding the Florida Panhandle, many people in the village began working jobs connected to the Naval Air Station in Pensacola. Milton, which is on the other side of the railroad tracks from Bagdad, is the home of Tanglewood. It was the closest place for my family to play golf.

At my house in Bagdad, there were hundred-year-old trees spread around our acre lot. Using just one club, I would hit it low to miss a limb or hit it high to get it over a limb. I would hit it one way or another to get around a bush or tree or an old lawnmower sitting in the grass. I used our aboveground pool as a water hazard. Most people who know me well are aware that I have played hundreds if not thousands of rounds with just one club. I've used anywhere from driver to sand wedge.

At Tanglewood our head pro when I was just starting to play, Hiram Cook, was a very good player. He had two kids and a wife who all played and loved the game. His daughter, Robin, who was a couple of years older than me, was one of the best junior girls in the area. In the afternoons after school, we would all play together. To make the matches fair, Hiram would play the round with just one club and use the forward tees with us. One week he might use a 7-iron and on another he may have a 6- or 7-iron. As I got older, I would ask him what he gained from using one club. He said that it taught him how to play different shots.

I had already been doing much of the same around my house. I would say that my mind is my best tool in many walks of life because I'm big on imagining things, seeing possibilities. I learn by watching and listening and doing. The more I practiced with one club, the more skillful I got at imagining different kinds of shots with every club in my bag. I was fortunate to learn the game the way I did. The process of self-discovery was ideal for my learning style. It turbocharged my development and helped my game improve faster than most kids did at that age.

I don't remember any amazing shots from that 62 in the Divot Derby. Most of what has stayed with me happened off the course. This was a life-changing event where golf now represented a real future for me. Newspapers were now writing about this kid who had just shot 62. When I showed up with my family a few nights later for the Divot Derby awards dinner at the New World Landing, an event space in Pensacola, I was on the top of the world. The dinner is the highlight of the local junior golf season. On jumbotrons they showed all the pictures from the tournament. After the ceremony we all went to play miniature golf at the local Goofy Golf, which had windmills and a twenty-foot-tall T-Rex dinosaur.

After closing down for several decades, a few years ago the Goofy Golf facility was purchased and restored by the local First Tee program for use as its headquarters. In 2017, I began hosting an annual mini golf tournament at the facility to support the First Tee's mission of growing the game while also helping kids develop life skills through golf. At the ribbon cutting I explained that I was so passionate about the facility because of what it had meant for me and my family. These were the moments that helped me love the game because of the smiles that it brought to my mom's and dad's faces and how it brought our friends together.

At the Divot Derby Champions Dinner, I just felt like I was the man. You feel like the man when you shoot 62. This is where a kid learns pride and ego. I was winning the younger division but I had my sights set on the bigger trophy. I started to have dreams of continuing to play and getting better and winning more trophies. Now my parents wanted to take me to more tournaments. We knew that I was good locally, but we needed to venture out to see how my games stacked up against the top juniors in the world.

This was a big moment for not just me but my whole family. My parents, who were working-class people, had always made sacrifices so that I could have the very best. After continuing to see improvement with my golf at six and seven years old, they decided that I needed some real equipment. It wasn't easy to find left-handed clubs, but I was fortunate to have a left-handed pro at my club. My dad had a terrible set of clubs. He never spent the money on himself, but he believed I should have the best of everything. It was a boatload of money for my parents, but for Christmas when I was eight years old, they bought me a PING junior set. I've played that brand ever since.

But Dad did have his limits. I didn't wear a golf glove until junior college, where I began to receive free equipment, because he thought they were too expensive. He also believed that you could feel the clubs better with your hands without a glove. It was a similar thing with the ball. He didn't want me to waste anything. He hated to see me throw a ball into the woods or a water hazard. Even though Titleist now gives me free balls, I have a tendency to use one ball for eighteen holes.

We ordered that first set of PING clubs through the company's local representative, Billy Weir, an older gentleman who called himself "the short, round man." He took a liking to me, I think, because he never had kids. My parents paid for the clubs, and every year as I got bigger, they would add more clubs until I was able to get a full set when I turned twelve. After the 62, Weir wrote a letter to his boss, the owner of PING, John Solheim, telling him about a left-handed kid who was shooting low scores with PING equipment. I continued to play PING through high school and college. Years later, after I turned professional,

Mr. Weir would introduce me to John Solheim, leading to my lifelong relationship with the family that founded the PING golf equipment company, but we'll dive into that more later on.

I stopped wearing knickers after I shot that 62. I still admired Payne Stewart, but I think that was the moment when I started to grow up. I had started wearing knickers when I was eight or nine. My grandmother, my father's mother, lived in a trailer in our backyard. She didn't drive or work, so I would go over to her house after school and she would make knickers for me to wear when I played golf. One year for the finals of the Drive, Chip and Putt at Disney in Orlando, she sewed Disney characters on my pants.

With my parents' blessing, the 62 also led me to focus more on golf and less on other sports, including baseball, my dad's favorite. I was a good baseball player, but I never played on an all-star team because it interfered with the start of golf season. My dream had been to be a New York Yankees pitcher who played first base, who on his off days from pitching hit home runs. Before shooting the 62, I was never seriously confronted with focusing exclusively on one sport. As a kid it depended on the day and my mood if I were a golfer or a baseball player. If I were a golfer, I would hit balls over and around the house, and if I were a baseball player, I bounced tennis balls off the roof to help me practice fly balls. My parents let my sister and me dabble in everything. My friends and I still played pickup basketball but not on competitive or travel teams because it took up too much time. I couldn't dribble but I had the touch to be a good shooter.

I didn't think of golf as a job, but I treated it as a job. I started traveling around the Southeast to play on the American Junior Golf Association Tour (AJGA), which is the top junior circuit in the world. I never won out there, but I usually finished in the top ten. For me, it became all or nothing. I began telling my schoolteachers that grades didn't matter because I was going to be a professional golfer. I think that's the reason why I had so many naysayers, because I had such a stubborn belief in myself. When people asked, "What happens if your plan doesn't work?" I would say, "It's going to work. There is no other option."

My dad used to always say you've got to be a leader or a follower, and you don't want to be a follower. He knew me better than I knew myself. "Bubba, you have two options," he would say. "You got to be really smart or really good at sports and you're not smart. So you better be really good at sports." He didn't say it in a negative way. That was just my dad's way of firing me up.

I still have the Titleist Balata ball that I used to shoot the 62 at the Divot Derby. I keep it in a case on a shelf in my house. It's old and dingy now but 62 is legible in black marker across the logos. I cherish this ball as much as any I've kept for a win. I was only thirteen years old but it felt like the peak of my career. At the time I thought, *Maybe this is as good as it's ever going to get.*

Two years after winning the twelve- to thirteen-year-old division and shooting the 62, I won the boys senior division of the Divot Derby, perhaps the most prestigious of the age groups, to join the ranks of Heath and Boo as the overall champion of the event. It marked my eighth year in a row of winning at the Divot Derby, but it didn't feel as significant as that victory from a couple of years earlier. My mindset is that I never know what's going to happen. In my first Masters in 2008, it was the only time that Boo, Heath, and I were ever together in the field. You never know if you are going to play in this tournament again that you have been wanting to play since you were a child. In life and golf you learn not to take anything for granted. I had just shot in the

60s for the first time in a tournament without a bogey. That was a number only professionals shot.

I felt like I had grown up. I had found my spot and my sport. From that moment forward, I was obsessed with being a golfer. There was no backup plan.

CHAPTER 3

Mom & Dad—Simple Wisdom from Complex People

Some have said I have a personality that is tough to read. I promise you I came by it honestly.

Leaning against a tree with a cigarette in one hand and a Styrofoam cup full of beer in the other is how my dad watched me play many junior golf tournaments. He wouldn't say much to the other parents. If he met them time after time at tournaments and saw that their son was regularly competing against me, he might begin to open up and talk . . . or he might not. Like many youth sports, golf families come from all walks of life: you had players with parents who had private jets, other parents who were doctors and lawyers, some who were businesspeople. Then there was my dad, who simply referred to himself as a construction worker at a chemical plant. There was a clique and he wasn't a part of it, nor did he seem to want to be a part of it. He was there for me, not for any of them.

Eventually, after a year or so, he began interacting with a few people that we saw at a lot of tournaments, but he always portrayed an image of being standoffish, OK not to "fit in." He never joined the huddles of parents bragging about their sons, preferring to watch his own from under the security of a shady tree, and my mom carried the same demeanor. I wasn't there from the very beginning of their marriage, so I don't know which one of them is most responsible for this trait, but I suspect it's my dad.

This wasn't just something he did at golf events. During my high school basketball games, Dad would stand against a wall with a frown on his face. He always stood out with his bright-colored Sansabelt pants that could be pink, yellow, red, or orange. Mom would always sit around one of the low corners of the bleachers to be near Dad, who would never sit because he was never comfortable with anyone being behind him. Still, he wanted to stay near her "just in case something crazy happened." For the record, nothing ever did. But that didn't stop him from imagining the possibility. His mind was different. In Vietnam he had seen things that most of us could never imagine, and there is no question it impacted him for the rest of his life. He was suspect about many things and didn't want to leave his back uncovered, but underneath that tough exterior was a man with a kind heart.

Dad showed that heart more to young people than to adults. One of my favorite examples: There was a kid in Bagdad who was about six-foot-seven and played basketball. He wanted to play point guard and shoot 3-pointers and fadeaway jumpers, but he couldn't do any of those things well. Raised by a single mom, he didn't have a strong male influence, so my dad brought the young man into our lives and tried to help him with his basketball skills and showed him how to use his whole arm when he threw a baseball. There were times when the kid went with us to the golf course. Dad knew how to be that male figure or just that person to step in when more love and support was needed, even though he didn't really want people to see that side of him.

Dad was a natural teacher and a man of high integrity. Instead of long sit-down speeches, he often conveyed important moral lessons in just a couple of sentences. "The only thing a poor man has is his word," he told me. "Never lie. I don't care how bad the truth is, never lie. Tell the truth. And here's a promise: I will never lie to you." But more important than just saying the words, he believed that you had to build trust with people through your actions. I learned how to treat a woman with love and affection by watching the way he treated my mother. He kissed my mom every day before he went to work and again when he got home.

My mom, who grew up the youngest of nine on a farm in Mississippi, was the cuddler and more outwardly affectionate parent. Every night as a child I would go to bed and my dad would say good night. Then my mother would come into my room and read me a story as she scratched my back with her long fingernails. They were often stories of athletes exercising courage or tenacity or some other trait that I as a young kid could take through life.

I never became much of a reader, and it would not have surprised me if I were diagnosed with a learning disability, but such things were not as commonly diagnosed back then. At the same time, I often did a pretty good job of hiding my struggles. For example, to ace spelling tests, I learned to memorize the list of words, but what people didn't know is that I couldn't read them on a piece of paper in sentences. I was very good at math, but I never liked to show my work, finding it easier to solve problems in my head. When I first started going to the golf course with my dad, I would irritate some of his friends because I kept their scores in my head. No golfer likes hearing their double bogey called out to the world, especially from a precocious little boy. Once my mom figured out that I really had a problem with reading, we discovered that I was a visual learner. That led her to work with me in a different way. She would place me in the stories that she read to me. She would say Bubba this and Bubba that, and I would be very interested and memorize everything about the story because I could visualize it.

My attitude toward school wasn't helped by the fact that, by high school, I was already envisioning a career in golf—and boldly proclaiming it to others. That didn't sit well with everyone. One teacher actually told my mom that I was not going to amount to anything.

After being offended, Mom decided to turn this into a chip I would carry on my shoulder for a very long time. "I guess you're going to have to show her differently," she told me.

In many ways, my mom, sister, and I were the second act of Dad's life. He was born in the Atlanta area but lived in Charlotte, North Carolina, before moving with his mother to Pensacola when he was in high school. He married his high school sweetheart, and they had a child. For a while he worked in construction with his stepdad. The marriage was troubled and when he got a divorce, his ex-wife notified the draft board (which at the time saw single men differently than those married with children), and they called his number in 1969 for the Army. Dad had earned a GED after dropping out of high school, but after being drafted and completing basic training, he took some tests and was admitted to Officer Candidate School, where he was commissioned as a Second Lieutenant.

During a tour in Vietnam, Dad was deployed in both Detachment B-36 (3rd Mobile Strike Force Command, or MIKE

Force) and the 5th Special Forces Group (Airborne). The Special Forces, or the "Green Berets," was created by the Army to wage guerrilla warfare. During the war, the primary mission of the US Special Forces was to advise the Civilian Irregular Defense Group, the Vietnamese paramilitary counterinsurgency force.

For several months in 1970, my father, who was by then a twenty-four-year-old First Lieutenant, was the executive officer with the 3 MIKE Force in the zone that oversaw the capital city of Saigon in south Vietnam. In Long Hai there was a training center where US Special Forces trained Cambodian soldiers in infantry tactics and intelligence to fight the Khmer Rouge, a Cambodian Communist-backed group. While out on patrol in Long Hai, Dad was struck by shrapnel from an exploding grenade. The shrapnel that was dislodged from his face left a scar under his right eye, but a piece of shrapnel that ended up too close to his kidney stayed in his body until after his death, when my mom had it removed. Dad didn't talk much about Vietnam. Even to the day he died, he would never give us many details, often saying simply that he had served in Asia or Europe.

Dad didn't like that he had been wounded, although he referred to it as being "hurt on the job." "I didn't do my job right," is what he would say. That's what the injury meant to him. He was entitled to be awarded a Purple Heart, but he wanted no part of that. "Why would I get an award for being injured? I should get an award for not being injured," he said.

After my dad left Vietnam, the commanding officer he had served under was killed in action. He certainly knew others who were killed or wounded but he didn't talk about that. Dad also worked Veterans Day every year. He never took that day off. "I got paid to do a job," he said, "so why should I get special recognition for it?" That was his mindset.

Dad met my mother after he came back from Vietnam. She had left Mississippi after graduating from Mississippi State, heading for the Pensacola beaches. Mom was working part-time as a bartender at a beer joint on the beach, hoping to earn enough to buy a new motor for her Volkswagen. Dad was just home from the war, and he was popular with many of the pilots training at the Naval Air Station who had questions about Vietnam. At my mom's bar there was a bumper pool table, where Dad would hold a beer in one hand and use his other hand to control the cue stick as he played.

When he came into the bar, he would flirt with Mom. "OK, girl," he would tell her, "one of these days it's going to be you and me." At first Mom wasn't interested in him, but he wore her down with his charm and eventually they started dating and were married in the spring of 1973.

I was born in 1978, three years after my sister, Melinda. When I came out of Mom's womb, my dad decided that I was going to become a pitcher for his favorite team, the New York Yankees. He had been a high school catcher and just plain loved the game of baseball. My parents believed that from the very beginning of my life I showed signs that I might become a good athlete with some special physical talents. My mother loves to tell the story of the time we were at a parade when I was about thirteen months old and she realized I had some gifts. My sister was in a stroller and Mom was holding me by my arms. A man on a float threw beads that struck me in the chest. I picked the beads up and threw them back at him. Mom went home and told my dad what had happened. By then I was showing signs that I was left-handed. My mom was so convinced that I was going to be a pitcher for the Yankees that she wrote Yankees owner George Steinbrenner a letter to tell him the story too.

Dad wasn't much of a golfer. Before I was born, he played some with another Vietnam veteran, Phillip Durant, who was the older brother of Joe Durant, a four-time PGA Tour winner and a local golf legend around Pensacola. When Joe was ten, he would tag along with the two Vietnam vets as they played a local par-3 course. One day my dad told Joe that if he beat him, he was going to sell his clubs. After Joe did just that, my dad went out the next day and sold his clubs. He didn't pick up a club again until I was about six years old.

My mom made Dad take me to the golf course with him on Saturday mornings to meet his buddies from work. In the beginning I was mostly interested in what it would be like to drive the golf cart, but I quickly picked up the game once the club pro found me a left-handed club.

As I grew to enjoy the game, Mom started joining us out on the course. Some of those who saw us thought that my mother was babying me by carrying my bag when I played. They thought that I should carry my own bag, but my mom, who seldom got to spend time with me on the course because she worked long hours in banking, enjoyed the time walking with me and helping me out where she could. In the summers, Tanglewood became a "babysitter" for my sister and me. Mom would drop us off in the morning and Dad would pick us up in the evenings, and we would literally spend the day there on and around the course. I was learning the game and having a lot of fun, but I didn't take it very seriously. Even when I was beginning to win some of the local events, I had more fun putting on trick shows around the putting green after the tournament.

Some around Tanglewood told my parents that if they wanted me to become a "real" golfer that our family would need to move over on the course. My parents listened, but they still went ahead and followed their own path for helping me grow in the game. When everybody was getting golf lessons, they didn't make me get them just because other people thought that it was the right thing to do. My dad would encourage me to play instead of beating balls on the driving range. On the drive home after every tournament, it was always about what you could take from the experience and what you could improve upon for the next time. I was eleven when my parents first let me travel to a tournament without them. I caught a ride with my idols Boo Weekley and Heath Slocum, who were five years older than me and had their driver's licenses. When I got home that night, my parents asked me what I had learned during the tournament. "I learned that Boo can kill an armadillo with a golf club," I said. That wasn't what they expected to hear. But what I learned most came from watching and listening.

Taking me to all those tournaments placed a financial strain on my parents but they never let me know. I know that we, as a family, lived on a pretty tight budget. That meant we didn't take the more expensive trips that required air travel. When I was about fifteen and we didn't have the money or time to travel to some of the top American Junior Golf Association tournaments, my mom learned about a local weekend series that was sponsored by a beer company. Instead of competing against my peers around the country, I went head-to-head with many of the better adult golfers from the Florida Panhandle. My dad loved the series because after each tournament the sponsor provided free beer. Perhaps my dad had his own motives for wanting to stick around after the tournaments, but what he made sure I learned from playing in those events is that no matter how bad you played, you always stuck around and talked to others. I was competitive in the series and for a couple of years I finished near the top of the points race.

This was golf for my dad, sticking around to support me with a beer and a cigarette to help him pass the time while I was on the course. Besides his annual company tournament, he rarely played golf once it really became my game. In his mid-forties, he quit the game completely after developing rheumatoid arthritis. Around the time I turned pro in the early 2000s, the arthritis became crippling for him. One of his big toes began curling under his foot, which made it difficult for him to walk. It was weird to watch his physical transformation over this period. He had been a strong and robust man who played softball and basketball. It was a shock to him and everybody in and around our family to see him hobbled as he was by his own body betraying him.

———

While I always knew Dad was there to protect us, the one thing about growing up in a community like Bagdad during my childhood was that it almost always felt safe. From very early on I would walk myself to my elementary school. At five years old I began riding my bicycle all over town. I went from house to house visiting friends. On Saturday mornings I would stop by the Volunteer Fire Department and hang with the guys while they washed the trucks, told stories, and cooked breakfast.

I don't remember what I did to deserve a punishment, but one time I wasn't allowed to ride my bike for a week. There was a small convenience store down the street from our house. Dad stopped by the store one day after work to buy cigarettes. At the counter, the owner said to him, "I see that your boy had to ride his sister's bike because his must be broken."

When my dad got home, he said, "Bubba, didn't I tell you not to ride your bike?" "I didn't," I said. "I rode Melinda's bike." That didn't go well.

My dad never was a stern taskmaster. He and Mom trusted me always to do the right thing. My love of old-school hip-hop was heavily influenced by the freedom they gave me to roam the streets of Bagdad. As a ten-year-old, I would go on Sunday afternoon bike rides to a softball field, where mostly African American teams held their games. They would cook hamburgers and hot dogs and play music. As I got older, they would let me retrieve the foul balls that were hit outside the fence. For hours, I would just sit with my baseball glove, hoping that they would ask me if I wanted to play. Finally, a few years went by and they did let me play.

I always knew the games were about to start when I heard the music bumping from car stereos. I could hear from my house the bass, the beat, and the rhyming lyrics as cars drove by with the loudness of ten-inch subwoofers in their trunks. These beats got stuck in my head as I caught tennis balls off our slanted roof or hit plastic golf balls around the house. I filled my first tape player with hits by Run DMC, the Beastie Boys, Grandmaster Flash, and the Sugar Hill Gang. I would go to bed listening to one side of a tape and the next night I would listen to the backside. The Run DMC Christmas album was one of my favorites. The music just became part of me, and I carried it in my head everywhere I went, much like the lessons I learned from my father and mother.

If the foundation of life, of your personality, of your nature, is framed by what you saw at home and then colored by what you learned from the community around you, then it's no surprise that I grew up to be a bit of an outsider. I was unwilling to trust strangers, happy to do things my own way while believing that all that truly matters is telling the truth, doing the right thing, and loving those closest to you. That is the example my parents set for me. It seemed simple, until it wasn't.

CHAPTER 4
A Youth in Golf

At some point during my senior year in high school, my dad and I developed this vision of me turning pro. But not just turning pro eventually. I was going to turn pro right after I graduated from high school!

It wasn't necessarily a good vision—it didn't feel like God's plan for me or anything like that—but we felt like it was a solid plan. We didn't seek the opinions of people we knew or call a family meeting to discuss it. It was based on a pretty simple set of facts: I did not like school and wanted to do nothing else but play golf, and my dad didn't place a whole lot of stock in the value of a college education. So, there it was.

I wasn't thinking specifically about joining the PGA Tour at the age of nineteen, just about continually improving, and taking my game to the professional level—whatever that actually meant—seemed like a logical next step. Most likely, I would end up playing in mini tour events, maybe hoping one day to join the big Tour. Most people are unaware that it's a lot easier to turn professional in golf than in most other sports, if getting "paid to play" is what you mean by professional. When you're ready, you just say, "I'm a pro." Then you sign up, pay an entry fee, and compete for cash in small tournaments called the mini tours with other guys who hope to join the Tour someday too.

Back then, once a year, everybody also got to compete in something called "Q School," which was an event designed for aspiring PGA players. The top finishers in Q School got a PGA Tour card. Dad and I felt that if I entered enough mini tournaments and competed in Q School, eventually I would earn my card.

Besides, some of the bigger mini tours themselves paid out around $20,000 to the winner. And twenty grand for a week's work . . . it was a big payday for my family.

From those vantage points, our "vision" made all the sense in the world. I was, in my mind, meant to be a golfer. That had never been in doubt since shooting that 62 at the Divot Derby.

Since Randall lived all of 100 yards from the Tanglewood clubhouse, his house was basically our home base. We never hung out at my house. If Randall and I weren't golfing at Tanglewood, we would play at Stonebrook, which was considered a "nicer" venue than Tanglewood. Randall's mom worked in the pro shop at Stonebrook, and he worked as a cart boy there from the time he was fourteen until his last year of college. As for me, well, I never worked a real job in my entire life. Not once. As I said, I had my path laid before me and that pathway was inside the ropes.

When we weren't playing golf, which wasn't too often, we played tennis or basketball in Randall's driveway. We would also hang out at the pool where both of our sisters spent time working as lifeguards. With a pool, tennis courts, and clubhouse, in addition to a golf course, Tanglewood was technically a "club," but it wasn't a glamorous one, as was evidenced by its nickname, Tangle*weed*.

Randall and I both went to Hobbs Middle School. We didn't have a big group of friends, not because we were unpopular or antisocial, but because when you're in the habit of getting up at seven a.m. every Saturday to play two rounds of golf, you're not thinking of socializing. But we weren't complete hermits and often went to football games on Friday nights under the lights and basketball games in the winter.

I also played a lot of golf with people who were older than me. As a result, I heard and participated in a lot of "adult" conversations about people, jobs, money, retirement, and so on during our rounds. This had an impact on me, too, just as my own parents did.

I think the biggest impact was to help me see life in a longer-term way than a lot of other kids my age. I could see how you had to have a vision for your life and do everything in your power to be true to your vision. You could stay true to it by making good decisions and not taking the easy way out. For me, the easy way would have been to goof around more and sneak out on a Friday or Saturday night to go drinking. But I chose not to for at least two reasons: first, because frankly, I never understood why getting drunk and feeling sick was supposed to be fun, and second, that party might look tempting, but I had somewhere else I needed to be in twenty years' time. If it sounds like I never got to be a kid, that wasn't the case. I was as goofy as they came and still am. But I was wired for regular improvement more than anybody else I knew.

I was an unconventional golfer even in middle school and high school. If I got in the woods, I wouldn't measure the odds of hitting it out and decide to play it safe and chip it to the fairway. I'd go for it and hammer it out with a lofted club. People thought it was the wrong approach, which meant they saw my game as less safe. That led more than a few folks to predict I wouldn't be successful.

In addition to being seen as an overly aggressive player, a lot of people thought my technique would eventually limit my development. What they didn't understand is that my technique was nothing more than an effort to work with what I had. I later realized that my golf equipment didn't fit my body. I've always had long arms and big hands, and by high school I was swinging pretty hard. The standard-size grips on my clubs were way too small for my hands and the shafts in my clubs were too "whippy," or flexible, for my powerful swing, but I didn't know it back then. The combination of small grips and whippy shafts meant it was a lot easier to hit the ball when I played a massive hook for most of my youth. I never thought of playing that hook as a big deal or major innovation at the time. However, when I got to college, I began to play equipment that was specifically for me, with larger grips and stiffer shafts. This helped me eventually unlearn a few of the habits I developed back then. For example, after playing a massive hook for most of my youth, by the time I was in my early twenties I had started playing a slice, curving the ball the other way on nearly every tee shot. But I've always been an instinctive player who had the ability to bring a club around the way I wanted to, whether it was to hit a ball high or drive it low or bend it, or what have you.

As I got older, I increasingly began to do a lot more traveling to tournaments put on by the American Junior Golf Association. I loved winning trophies and wanted to win more of them. Most of all, I wanted to get outside of the local community and travel to where the best players were playing. My parents supported my desires and began seriously looking at tournaments in the Atlanta area and even in Mississippi, places where we'd have to stay overnight. Gradually, in order to make this work, I cut back on playing baseball. I kept playing during the regular season but dropped out once All-Star teams were picked and traveling was required. This didn't sit particularly well with my dad, but it would have been hard for him to argue against keeping my foot on the pedal with the success I was having with golf.

I continued to play on the Milton High School golf team and enjoyed playing with my friends and classmates. Milton had a proud golfing tradition, having recently graduated Boo Weekley and Heath Slocum, who along with me would become known as "the big three of Milton," but my focus was on the national junior tourneys. Even though I didn't win a single one, I moved up as high as number three in the national rankings.

Yes . . . the plan my father and I had hatched up seemed to be unfolding very nicely. The vision seemed attainable. And then, two conversations occurred that put the kibosh on all visions of "going pro," at least in the near future.

––––––

The first conversation was with my mom. Unlike "natural born" Watsons who never made it past high school, let alone college, she had in fact graduated both from high school and college and wanted her son to graduate from both as well. I don't remember my parents arguing about this, but I'm pretty sure I know how the conversation went because a couple days later my mom sat me down and said, "Bubba, I know you love your golf and I want you to enjoy all the success in the world with it, but I spoke to your father and you're going to get a college education. End of discussion."

Well, the decision was made but it turned out that it wasn't exactly the end of discussion. Oh, I was going to college alright. Of that, there was little doubt. The question was, *How was I going to go to college?* My dad had already let me know that he had no intention of paying for my college education, but I had an even more pressing problem than financing. And that brings us to the second conversation.

Around this time, I went in to meet with my guidance counselor and was told, in no uncertain terms, that I was in serious danger of failing high school and not graduating. "If you don't start taking your classes seriously and working harder, Bubba, you're not going to graduate. And that means you can also forget about playing golf in college," she said. When I explained to her that I had no intention of going to college because I was going to play professional golf, she dismissed the idea outright and told me going pro was a "one-in-a-million shot" and unlikely to play a part in my future.

I've thought a lot about this conversation over the years and have come to believe she wasn't trying to be mean or shoot me down. Maybe she thought she was doing me a favor by giving it to me straight about my odds going pro and hoped to save me from future disappointment. One thing was for sure, she seemed quite sure that I was on a path to failure and there would be nobody to blame but myself.

My first thought was, *Where in blazes are you coming from?* I had never failed a single class in my life, so how could I not graduate? Yes, my GPA was a paltry 1.9, but that wasn't failing. My second thought was more or less the same one I always had whenever I felt somebody was doubting me: *I'll show her! I'm going to work hard and become a professional golfer someday.* The point of relating this story is not to show how wrong my guidance counselor proved to be, but to offer an insight into the way my mind worked back in those days and in the years that followed. It was a stubborn, single-minded focus on proving myself that blinded me to other matters, important matters I should have been taking care of.

Like schoolwork.

I grew up with this understanding between my parents and me: I was supposed to be a leader, not a follower, and I was supposed to achieve something either by being smart or by being good at sports. At some point early on in my childhood, we decided that my best shot would be in sports, not brains, and my responsibility was to make it my passion in life and become a leader in it. If I could manage my talent to get a free ride in college, my parents would take care of the rest.

And they did. While we were a blue-collar family, both of my parents worked. My mom even took on a paper route as a second job to help pay for expenses. As a result, while my dad always played with cheap clubs that weren't very good, I always had nicer clubs. And while we didn't take vacations that required long-distance flights, when it became obvious that my game had improved to the point that we needed to travel to where the cream of the crop played, that's where we went, even if it meant traveling and staying overnight somewhere.

Though my grades weren't anything to brag about, I wasn't stupid. What I was, was totally unmotivated in the classroom. By the time I was a senior, my GPA wasn't good enough to get me into a four-year university. For subjects that involved reading and taking notes and writing essays, I had no time. I didn't mind subjects I had a natural inclination for, like math, which I could do fairly well in my head. But even with math, I never wanted to show my work, and this worked against me. As a matter of fact, my ability to hold lots of numbers in my head worked against me on the golf course as I'd developed the irksome habit of keeping everybody's score in my head and calling them out after each hole. "Okay, Randall's a six for that hole. Tommy's a five, and I'm a four."

When I was interested in something, there was nobody who would get more information about that topic than me. The topic might be about an athlete or musician, but it also might be science or business. I'd look for information from a specific person or by listening to other people who were talking about something I thought interesting. One of the things I'm known for is being self-taught on the golf course. My dad offered me a few tips, of course, but nothing like the kind of close analysis of a swing that coaches look at. I think this spilled over from golf into life. I honestly believed that I didn't need anybody's highly paid help to learn about the things that interested me. Like my mom and dad, I had plenty of common sense to apply to any problems I might encounter. Today, I look back and believe that I was shooting myself in the foot by thinking this way. But you know what they say about hindsight.

The truth is, when you tell the whole world (at least the whole world of Bagdad) that you're going to be a professional golfer, you set yourself up for a lot of negative blowback. And when you remind people, as I often did through my attitude, that you plan to do it your own way—and not take any lessons, for example, or play conservative shots—you invite even more naysayers into the ring. That was me—I was about as unconventional as they came and far too proud of it.

CHAPTER 5

"Go Dawgs!"

Every now and then, the God of second chances shows his face to us, and we get the opportunity to erase a mistake we've made in our lives. When this occurs, the only real question is whether we have the wisdom or instinct to grab on to the opportunity and hold on for dear life. When it was clear that I wasn't going to get into any four-year colleges, a minor miracle happened.

A man I knew named Chris Haack, who used to run the American Junior Golf Association back in the day when I was playing in it, was offered a coaching position at the University of Georgia. This happened not long before I was set to graduate from high school. One day, I received a recruitment call from Coach Haack, who told me he'd been watching me improve over the years and liked my approach to the game. Would I be interested in coming to play for him at Georgia? I told him, well, yes, I would be very interested; but when I told him about my grades, he had the same kind of response I'd grown accustomed to hearing.

"Oh, that will never get you into Georgia, Bubba, not to mention qualifying for a scholarship." The truth was that not only did I need a scholarship to attend college, I needed a full ride.

But our conversation wasn't over just yet, because then Coach Haack said, "Bubba, I know your grades are terrible, and you won't qualify for a scholarship right now. But if you spend a couple years in junior college, put in some real work in the classroom, and keep playing golf, I'll hold a full scholarship for you when you're ready. You can come play for me at Georgia and also get the opportunity to play once a year at Augusta National Golf Club. What do you think?"

What did I think? "Game on!" is about the closest thing that came to mind. It was true that growing up, whenever I actually thought of myself going to college, it was always to Florida State University. My parents and I used to watch FSU football games on television, and one of my heroes was the great Seminole linebacker Derrick Brooks, from Pensacola. I wanted to be the Derrick Brooks of golf and even thought about having his number, 55, stitched on my shirt. When a representative from FSU's golf program joined the group of schools that tried to recruit me in high school, I felt proud, but there was no way FSU was going to take me with my grades.

Georgia wasn't exactly a second-rate school either, not by a long shot. In my senior year in high school, Georgia won the national championship in golf. They were a legitimate top ten golf program. Coach Haack was one of the better college coaches around. He won two national championships in 2000 and 2005 and was runner-up in 2007 and 2011. Coach told me that from his perspective, he'd just as soon talk to an "older" fellow like me than a high school sophomore sitting there quaking on the couch. The way he saw it, if I could apply myself in junior college and come to Georgia, he would likely get two good years out of me. Otherwise, he'd have to take a chance on bringing in a freshman who would be scared to death and require a year or two to compete. So the coach's call lit a fire under my underachieving backside to get good grades and earn the chance to see how I stacked up against the guys in a national program.

My mom and I made some inquiries and found a junior college called Faulkner State Community College in nearby Baldwin County, Alabama, that said they'd take me. "Oh, and you can play on our golf team," they didn't forget to mention. I remember the Faulkner State coach came out to watch me one day when I was playing in a tournament at Kiva Dunes Golf Club. It was a professional tournament in which I shot a 67 as an amateur and finished second. The coach had me sign on the dotted line that afternoon. I enrolled at Faulkner and took classes on Monday, Wednesday, and Friday. No sooner had I began practicing with the golf team, however, than I immediately complained to the coach that I wasn't learning anything at practice. My teammates were "too far behind me."

The coach reminded me of how important it was to be a team player and for us to practice as a team as well as compete against other colleges as a team. He was 100 percent right, of course, but I felt I'd get more out of it if I went home and played with my guys. (I know: Bubba the knucklehead at it again.) I proposed to the coach that if I could get a better score on our home course than anybody else on the team without using any woods—my 4-iron would be my longest club—could I train without my teammates? He shook his head, but he agreed. I got the best score. And I stopped going to practice. I wasn't trying to be mean or hateful, but looking back, I know it must have been hurtful to the other guys to have the best player on their team snub them like that.

I did go on to become a junior college All-American but I was selfish and disrespectful. People say you have to be a little selfish and super confident to set yourself apart from other great golfers, but I seemed to take it to a new level. My schoolwork was good enough that I could have applied to FSU and maybe earned a scholarship, but by that time FSU had some guys on the team I wasn't interested in playing with. The rich kids. I mean, how immature could I be?

This period of my life was so full of *what ifs* that I can only explain it as God's plan for me. I made a lot of irrational and selfish decisions, but looking back, this period somehow set me on the path I needed to find. If I wasn't so immature and had gone to FSU, I wouldn't have met my beautiful wife at Georgia. And we wouldn't have gone on to experience the joy of raising two beautiful children. God has a plan for us, and the best thing we can do is not second-guess it. Let it happen.

The one thing I did know for sure was that my parents had promised me that if I worked hard and got a free college education because I was smart or athletic, they'd take care of the rest. We all held up our ends of the bargain. While some might argue I didn't get as good an education as I should have, that's on me.

At Georgia I was an All-American in my first year, which was my junior year of school. The highlight of that year was probably winning the Chris Schenkel Invitational with a score of 13-under, which is still good enough for third all-time best tournament score at Georgia. After the success of my junior year, my senior year proved rather disappointing. Early on in the season, before we started playing competitive matches, Coach Haack came up to me and told me that I wouldn't be traveling with the team to compete. There were five guys who were better than I was, and I was the sixth best. When I pushed him on this a little bit, he added that the other five guys had developed a great chemistry with one another and enjoyed traveling together. "They're playing really well now," my coach said.

Had I managed to alienate myself from my UGA teammates, just as I had in junior college, I wondered? I felt that I had been playing just as good as anybody else. Our whole team played in two tournaments, and I placed second in both. But there is more to being on a team than just playing good golf. I thought about the incident with Ryan Hybl, who was a friend of mine growing up who became the number one recruit in the country. When he was scheduled to pay a recruitment visit to Athens, I skipped town and went to play golf in North Carolina. I suppose I should have known better, but I knew how much he loved UGA and wanted to come and play golf there, and I didn't think I needed to stick around to sell him on UGA.

The following week, the coach was furious with me. "Where were you?!" he said. I told him, "There's nothing to worry about. Ryan's been dreaming of coming to Georgia since he was a kid. Don't get so worked up about it." Well, once again I had failed to step into the other fellow's shoes. Of course the coach would get worked up about it: doing everything humanly possible to bring in the best recruits was his job and would ultimately make or break his career. Although Ryan wound up coming to Georgia and bringing honor to the program by twice being named an All-American and All-SEC golfer, I knew my coach was disappointed in me for not doing more to welcome him to campus.

And then there was an NCAA finals tournament where I defied Coach Haack's order of not trying to reach the green on a difficult par-5 hole in two shots, a hole in which I missed a short putt that would have qualified us for match play and a shot at another national championship. We missed the cut by one shot.

In my senior year, I got to play in the Chris Schenkel because

I was the defending champion. But besides that, I spent the rest of the season watching my teammates, Erik Compton, Nick Cassini, Bryant Odom, David Miller, and my old pal Ryan Hybl, win seven tournaments. The team did well that year but failed to win the NCAAs with me sitting on the bench. Years later after I won the Masters, Coach Haack was quoted in the *Augusta Chronicle* saying that not playing me in 2001 "might have been the biggest bonehead mistake" on his part.* But the reality was, he had six really good players, and the five guys who played were third team All-American or better. Someone had to sit out, and I gave him reasons not to play me, even though I usually outplayed everybody in practice and beat them all at a couple of tournaments where I got to play as a "sixth" man.

Part of me wishes I'd been more mature and sat down with my coach and talked it through—found out why I wasn't playing in my senior year as a pre-season All-American. But I don't think I could have handled the answer back then, whatever it was. I just don't. In the end, I bit my tongue and made a decision I remain proud of to this very day: I stayed on the team. Looking back, I am sure Coach would not have been surprised if I had used the news that I was not going to play as a reason to quit the team and school. My parents were also emotional about the news and told me emphatically that I should quit school and turn pro. "Why stay at school if you're not going to get the high-level competition?" they asked. "Isn't that what you're there for?"

My own reply was to say, "Nope, I'm going to stay on the team and go to practice every day and beat every one of those five guys

* Scott Michaux, "Bubba Watson Saw Little Action as Georgia Golfer," *Augusta Chronicle*, April 2, 2013, https://www.augusta.com/masters/story/news /bubba-watson-saw-little-action-georgia-golfer.

in practice." Part of me believed that I might be able to win the coach back over to me if he saw me grinding like everybody else on the team; but another part of me just wanted to push myself to get better and prove myself once again. I stuck it out and did, in fact, outplay the rest of the team in practice on a daily basis.

Who knows: if I had not been motivated by being sidelined at UGA, maybe my golf career would have turned out very different. In some ways, the setbacks I faced early on created and fueled my desire to prove everyone wrong, and without that drive I might have given up on my dream long before reaching the PGA Tour. I like to believe it was just all part of God's plan for me.

And best of all, by not dropping out, I got to meet Angie and learn another great lesson: sometimes it was good to say no to your parents.

One of the highlights of my Georgia years was going to play at Augusta National, where the Masters Tournament is played. We played two months before the Masters, so it was wet there and the conditions weren't optimal, but it was Augusta National. The older guys on the team really hyped it up. I remember that everybody went out and bought a new outfit to wear, ironed it, and didn't touch it until game day. "You want to be *clean* when you play Augusta," they said. The guys counted down the days to play and watched the weather like hawks. The veteran players kept saying that as soon as you got on Magnolia Lane, with all of those gorgeous overhanging trees, your mind would be officially blown. I tried to downplay it like the tough college dude I thought I was, but as soon as we got to Magnolia Lane, I became like a little boy again. I just started snapping pictures until I ran out of film.

My first shot ever there I plugged it trying to get over the fairway bunker on one. I made a double bogey on the first hole. All I could think was, *Can I go back to the tee and start over?* After kicking myself a while for blowing my first hole, I settled down and eventually birdied the last hole to shoot a respectable even par 72. I felt good about being able to come back from opening up my round with a double bogey and finishing even par for the day. I was still an "innocent kid" and didn't have a lot of people and cameras to contend with, but there was the pressure of competing well against your teammates at a major course. Over the years, I don't think I've shot very many rounds over par at Augusta, so maybe that day was a sign of things to come.

Because my life never moves in a perfect straight line, the spring of 2001 wasn't exactly the end of my story at UGA. It turned out that in order to graduate from Georgia, I needed to take another semester of classes the following fall. However, during the summer leading up to that last fall, I had turned professional and found myself earning a lot of money playing golf—at least, a lot by my standards back in the day. I kept playing professional golf but also returned to school, only to find myself three credits shy of being able to graduate. So, when Christmas break rolled around and Angie and I talked about what our plans were for the coming months, I told her I was throwing my lot in with the mini tours. I was finished with school, once and for all.

She was disappointed I didn't graduate, but she also knew how badly I wanted to devote myself to golf. Well, after a few years on tour, in 2008, I got an unexpected letter from Coach Haack. He had heard and read of my bitterness at how things played out at Georgia and wanted to clear the air. His gesture was a bighearted and welcome one for me, not only because I don't like holding onto bad feelings, but also because I was beginning to entertain ideas of holding junior clinics and tournaments to help young people who were just coming into the game. I felt that if I was going to tell kids that getting their education was important, I'd better complete my own education at Georgia. So I called my old coach and told him that I wanted to graduate. I let him know that he didn't owe me any explanation for why he didn't play me. I was very frank with him about feeling hurt by my omission, but I assured him I was over it.

"Can you ask around the university and find out what I need to do to graduate and earn my degree?" I asked him. Coach Haack was very warm and told me how happy he was that I called him. "I know your senior year was a difficult time, and I'm sorry you had to go through a tough time." We agreed that it would be a win-win for everybody—Georgia and Bubba.

I met with a dean from the college, and we figured out what I needed to do to complete my degree in consumer economics. Fortunately, it didn't require classroom time, which I couldn't have afforded to take. The requirements were for me to write a long paper on consumer economics and then take a comprehensive exam of the major. I was able to work on these largely on my own, and, happily, during those periods when I needed to come to Athens to do research or take the exam, I ended up staying at Coach Haack's house, which was very helpful. I do remember feeling like quite the old dude sitting in that classroom taking the final exam. After it was over, the teacher asked me whether I wanted to know my grade or whether I had passed or failed.

"Are you kidding me?" I said. "Just tell me whether I passed, and I'll be on my way!" She told me that I'd passed, and later on

I received an invitation to walk with the other graduates during the commencement ceremony. I decided not to, even though I was immensely proud of earning my degree.

As usual, Angie hadn't pulled any punches when it came to encouraging me about going back and earning my degree. Not graduating from college when I was there never sat well with her, and her feeling was that it hadn't sat well with me either. Of course, she was dead-on about my feelings of guilt over my decision to turn pro before earning my degree. Once I did earn it, I felt as though I'd plugged a big hole in my life. I wanted Georgia to be a major part of our family. My wife graduated from Georgia, too, and I enjoy going back and playing in the golf team alumni tournaments. I immediately put the Georgia G logo on my golf bag, which I refused to do at previous alumni gatherings until I earned my diploma.

These days, when I see Coach Haack, I thank him for making me a tougher person, for helping me learn how to play inside myself. If you're going to reach the top of your game, you have to get in the flow and be in the moment and believe that nobody can beat you. That isn't an easy mental state to get into. It takes a certain toughness that comes from losing as well as winning, and always trying to learn something from your wins and losses. At Georgia I learned how not to be afraid of any other player. This didn't mean I didn't think highly of them as players. Only that when I played my best there was no way on earth any of them could beat me. If I didn't feel that way, I thought, I was just going through the motions. Then it's time to retire.

As a dad who has coached his eight-year-old boy's baseball team, I believe in this kind of competitive mindset. It's not about winning at all costs with kids but about stepping up to the plate and swinging. I teach the kids to err on the side of swinging for the ball, telling them what my dad told me, and what probably a million other dads tell their sons: "It's always better to strike out swinging than strike out looking."

But I also learned another lesson at Georgia, one about being a good teammate and even something about servant leadership. Golf is such an individual game that it's easy to forget how rewarding it is to be a part of a team, a group of guys you form close bonds with, bonds that can last forever. Even though I didn't get to play with the guys as a senior, I always felt close to them because of our experiences together in my junior year. The long rides to play in tournaments. Goofing around together. Going out for meals as a team. Playing Augusta and feeling like we were on top of the world. I may not have known how to show it back then, but I cared about them and wanted them to care about me. In recent years I have gotten better about touching base with some of my old teammates, something I should have done from the start. Despite the ups and downs of being on the team, I feel the college team experience is one of the reasons I have always loved playing in team events like the Ryder Cup and Presidents Cup. While I picked golf in part because it was an individual sport, it is nice to be on a team at times.

A few years after I got on the PGA Tour, one of my old teammates, David Miller, invited me to play with him at Letterman Day at UGA. Letterman Day is an annual event when guys who lettered in golf at Georgia come back to campus and pair up with old teammates for a little tournament. The alumni get the full run of Georgia's golf course for the day. The first time I went, my goal was to show my old teammates that I cared about them. I made sure to pick up the flags after we'd putted or I'd run over to the other side of the green to pick up a club somebody forgot about. I made it my mission to do whatever I could to make everybody feel comfortable and close. All the guys from my junior year were there: Nick Cassini and Bryant Odom and many others. David and I played together as a team. We had a blast reconnecting, and I believe that David and I won that day.

In 2015, I was devastated to hear that David passed away in his sleep from an unknown condition, leaving behind a wife and two kids. On the day David passed, I was just about to start playing in the Arnold Palmer Tournament and received a text from David's wife telling me what happened. "The funeral is in two days," she told me. There was absolutely no way I wouldn't be at David's funeral, so I called Arnold Palmer and explained to him that I was going to have to withdraw from his tournament. His reply showed the kind of class I always knew he had. He said, "Oh my gosh, Bubba. Do you need any help? I feel so bad. I'm so sorry for that family. For you. But you're doing the right thing. Being there like this always takes priority over a golf tournament."

Over time, my relationship with the university has also gotten stronger. They've honored me "between the hedges" during football games at Sanford Stadium. But even better than this was winning my bet against Angie's former basketball coach, Andy Landers, by hitting a golf ball out of Sanford Stadium, the seventeenth-largest stadium in the world. Coach Landers didn't think I could generate the speed to loft the ball past every one of Sanford's 92,746 seats.

I won the right to sit on the women's bench against Louisiana State as Coach Landers's assistant coach. The Bulldogs won that key game, and it remains one of my favorite Georgia moments.

The other one would have to be winning my first green jacket at Augusta National. Georgia's archrival is Georgia Tech, a school that has produced a bunch of major winners with guys like Bobby Jones, Larry Mize, David Duval, and Stewart Cink. Georgia had never graduated a future winner of a major tournament. Until 2012. Each year, the winner of the Masters is awarded a green jacket (in addition to a lot of money). According to tradition, the previous year's winner, which in my case was the South African golfer Charl Schwartzel, is brought in to present the new winner with his jacket. I'd thought long and hard about what I'd say when the time came, and as Charl slipped the jacket over my shoulders, I said, "Go Dawgs!"

CHAPTER 6

Angie—the One

They say you don't get a second chance to make a good first impression. Thank God, Angie gave me that second chance.

The first time I met the woman who would become my wife I was playing in a pretty intense pickup basketball game while wearing a Georgia golf shirt, white mid-calf socks, black Nike Air Jordan shoes . . . and khaki shorts with pleats, held up by a black leather belt. Not a look that screams "cool" on any basketball court, especially one where the woman I was hoping to impress was sitting on the sidelines. At six-foot-four, she was about an inch taller than me and taller than anyone that I had ever dated. And by the way everyone talked to her, she had game. I must have looked goofy to her in that outfit.

Angie had been a forward on the Lady Bulldogs basketball team, the school's first recruit from Canada. At Georgia, she was a member of the 1999 Final Four team and the 2000 Southeastern Conference championship team. She was back in Athens to rehab a knee she had injured while playing as a rookie with the WNBA's Charlotte Sting.

There were six indoor basketball courts at the campus

recreational center. There was also a rock-climbing wall, a swimming pool, and a track, but I loved the game of hoops, so I often made my way to the basketball courts. The first court always had the best players and it progressed down from there to Court 6, which was where a guy in khaki shorts should have been playing. But that fall I played about every other day with a group of women from the Lady Bulldog basketball team and nobody could beat us. We ruled Court 1.

On this particular day as we were playing, it was hard to miss the tall blonde girl who came into the gym wearing a knee brace and walking on crutches. I recognized her from around campus. (Ironically, she had caught my eye long before. When a friend of mine and I made a pact at the beginning of the school year that neither of us would date anyone seriously that fall, I described having seen her and said that I wanted an "out" on the pact if I could date the tall blonde with the injured leg. I didn't even know her name at the time!)

There in the gym she had come to see her old teammates, not meet a guy. But that didn't stop me from joining them after the game when they went over to chat with her. As she was telling the girls about her injury, a loose basketball almost knocked her over. When the group started to laugh about the incident, she turned her attention to me as if to say I had no right to participate in a laugh at her expense. With a sharp look she said, "Who are you?"

I tried to act cool as I spit out my name, as if she should have known who I was.

As we started a new game, Angie was sitting in a corner and my phone was just blowing up with calls from friends and family. "Your phone keeps going off!" she yelled at me over the noise of the crowded gym. I was running up and down the court while also trying to joke with her. "I'm so popular," I said. She was not impressed with my humor. All she wanted to do was catch up with her former teammates, but I couldn't resist the opportunity to ask her questions after the game. At this point she didn't have a clue that I was a golfer about to turn pro in a few months. She didn't know that when I asked her about her experience playing pro ball that I might have been looking for some insight to help my own situation. She just knew that I was this dude who looked goofy on the basketball court and had an awkward way of showing her attention.

She gave the shortest answers possible to each of my many questions. I was making a bad attempt at flirting, having no idea that while I was wowed by her looks, she had a vision of what her future mate might look like, and I checked *none* of the boxes. I would later learn that the person she had in mind was a "non-hairy, 6'5" guy who weighed about 225 with a muscular build." I stood there and was zero for four. But in my mind she had the ideal look for me.

The next time I saw her was over at the campus golf course where she was playing golf with her roommate, Mary Beth, whom I did not know. Today avid UGA fans may know Mary Beth as the wife of UGA football coach Kirby Smart. At the time, Mary Beth was on the basketball team, but they had only overlapped for a year, with Mary Beth being a freshman during Angie's senior year. Angie was staying with Mary Beth while she was at UGA for rehab.

They were teeing off on the tenth hole while I was on number one, which happened to be close to the tenth. I approached them and very coolly (in my opinion) asked if she wanted to play a round. She offered a not-so-enthusiastic yes and I turned to walk away, feeling pretty proud, when Mary Beth yelled for me to come back. She noted that I hadn't even asked for Angie's phone number, so she scribbled it on a corner of a golf scorecard and handed it to me. A few days later, we agreed to go back to play.

We met in the parking lot of the golf course. I didn't call it a date, but Angie considered it one. Weirdly, we were both nervous. Initially, she didn't understand fully what I meant when I said I was a golfer. In fact, she says she didn't actually "get" that I was on the UGA golf team until we started playing. The picture she had in her head of a golfer was her dad, who could barely break 95. I told her over the round about my aspirations of becoming a professional golfer and playing the PGA Tour. She liked my ambition because her dreams had always included high goals like making the Canadian Olympic team and playing in the WNBA.

Pretty quickly, Angie saw that I was more than just talk. On the first hole, I hit a long drive right down the middle, and then I hit my approach shot to about six inches from the hole and made birdie. But I wasn't out there to show off my skills. Mostly, I tried to help her with her swing. And I wanted her to get comfortable around my awkward self. Fortunately, by the eighteenth green I had made progress on both fronts.

She agreed to what I would argue was really our first date.

Two days after our golf outing came the "real" date—I consider it that because I got dressed nicely and drove over to pick her up. We ended up at the Longhorn Steakhouse in a booth for two, and the conversation just flowed. That's when, somehow, the subject of what kind of person she could see herself with came up and she offered her non-Bubba list. She then looked at me and asked, "What about you? What kind of woman would you see yourself with?"

"You," I said, not missing a beat. It could have turned awkward quickly, but somehow it didn't. When I took her home, we sat in the car and kept talking. I was a complete gentleman and walked her to the door.

After two weeks of more conversations and meals, she finally asked me: "Are you ever going to kiss me?" The rest is history.

———————

Even though Angie finally understood that I had actually been on the Georgia golf team, she didn't understand that only five players traveled to tournaments or that there was a very competitive process to make the lineup. She didn't know what it meant to be the sixth man in golf. In basketball if you're the sixth man you are the first person off the bench and you're going to get twenty to thirty minutes a game. It wasn't until years later when I was a successful PGA Tour player that she ultimately understood what a tough time I was having in my golf career when we met. That senior season was the first time things really hadn't gone my way since I was a kid.

I don't watch a whole lot of golf on television now, but back then I spent a lot of time watching tournaments. Angie had thought that the game was boring and too slow when her dad would plop down in front of the TV on Sunday afternoons to watch tournaments. But when she began dating me it became something that we regularly did together. Through watching tournaments with me, she became much more knowledgeable about the game and some of the best players in the world and what set them apart from others. She loved how actively I was studying those players, looking for hints at what I might be able to do when my day arrived.

As an elite athlete in her own right, Angie understands what it takes to be the very best. Ironically, our bond as athletes has also been a source of friction. She was an athlete who had to scrap for every ounce of gain that she got in the game of basketball. In her world, if you are struggling with free throws, you go and stand at the line and practice shooting for hours. When I would miss a cut in a tournament or generally wasn't playing well, she thought that I should be on the driving range hitting balls for hours or on the practice green with putting aids. But I never felt I could improve by hitting the range or going to the gym or talking to sports psychologists and coaches. That's never been my style. Early in our marriage, these philosophical differences were a hindrance in our relationship. Although we had different perspectives on what I should be doing when I wasn't playing well, we shared a desire and drive to be the very best in our respective sports.

In January 2002, Angie signed a contract to play with a French professional team. I left Georgia in December and turned pro. If I didn't make it through the PGA Qualifying School (I didn't), I was going to play the mini tours, which are tournaments played in smaller cities with much smaller purses. To make that work, I was committed to playing as many weeks of the year as I could. Our lives were going in different directions and thousands of miles apart, but I thought our bond could survive a long-distance relationship. We could talk on the phone, and I believed the time away from each other would allow us to focus on our goals.

Angie had a different perspective. She wasn't sure if she had the time and energy to invest in a serious relationship at the time. She was facing the prospect of playing twelve months a year between Europe and the United States if she caught on with another WNBA team. So after a couple months of dating and before heading overseas, she called me on the phone to break off the relationship before it got too serious.

She said those words that nobody in love wants to hear: "Let's just be friends." Obviously that wasn't what I wanted, but it takes two to make a couple and I had to respect her choice. But I didn't have to give up! So I continued to work and stayed in touch, hoping she'd change her mind before her January departure.

You could argue I wore her down, but within a few weeks we decided to give a long-distance relationship a try, and I couldn't wait to visit Angie in France during breaks after I had turned pro. Fighting to keep that relationship intact was one of the best decisions of my life, because during those two years our connection really grew in strength. It was hard—really hard—because of time differences and, frankly, because neither one of us was really that much of a phone talker. Still, we did the work to stay together and all these years later the challenge of that time has benefited us. Sometimes now we can just sit next to each other, not say a word, and fill our tanks.

But during that window our careers started to go in different directions. My golf was getting better, but her dreams of having a professional basketball career were slipping away. She was never the same player after she blew out her knee the year we met at UGA. Injuries had presented challenges in her past—during her freshman year at Georgia, she had surgery on her right shoulder and two more surgeries on that same shoulder during her pro career.

It was one of the lowest times in her life when she came to the realization that she wasn't going to have the WNBA career she had imagined or ever play for the Canadian women's Olympic team—in fact, the missed opportunity to play for her country in the Olympics still hurts when the topic comes up. Yet she was able to fill that void in her life by becoming a life partner to me in marriage in 2004, and a partner in our pursuit of a career on the PGA Tour.

As much as Angie and I shared a love of basketball and the quest of a career in pro sports, we could not have been more different when it came to our religious upbringings. I had almost no exposure to faith until my last year of high school, when I started attending Teen Nights at a local church.

I was raised in a non–church going family. My dad's family was indifferent to religion, an indifference that grew all the deeper in him after he went to Vietnam. He saw and experienced things there that made him question any God that would allow such travesty to happen. And Dad's attitude about going to church was one he shared openly: Why would he want to go to a place where people said they were there for God, but then spent so much time talking about each other behind their backs? My mom had grown up going to church, but by the time she met my dad in her early twenties, she no longer regularly attended services. So when my parents got married, church just didn't figure into their plans very often. They did send my sister and me to Sunday school, though what I mostly remember about that was the orange juice and donuts. We went to the main church service a couple of times, but never with our parents. There was no grace at the dinner table or prayers before bed.

During my senior year in high school, I became acquainted with two sisters who lived in my neighborhood. I would give them rides to school. On one of those drives to school, one of the girls randomly asked, "Hey, do you ever go to church?" When I told her no, she said, "All of your friends and a lot of my friends go to this church here in Bagdad." She invited me to the Teen Night on Wednesdays.

The youth pastor who organized these Teen Nights ended each evening with a little Bible study session. I started going regularly and remember one Bible study in particular, where I was suddenly overwhelmed by the joyous feeling that God loved me and that I was a good person. Not a good golfer, like the newspapers were always raving about. This was completely different. A good person. I listened to the youth pastor talk about how Jesus forgave us all for our sins and wanted us to be the best people we could be. In a way I can't really describe, I decided that a relationship with Jesus was one I wanted, and I chose to become a Christian. I cried the first time I closed my eyes and said a prayer, asking God to come into my heart. I continued to go every Wednesday until I went off to junior college in Alabama. Then gradually school and golf took over my life to the point where I stopped going to church altogether.

I couldn't tell you where in the world that girl from my neighborhood is today, what she did after high school, whether she got married or moved away or anything else. But I think of her with love and gratitude for planting a seed in me that continued to grow despite my own failures. Because God saved me, I came to understand that I was not only lucky to grow up the way I did, but also a bit blessed.

Angie, on the other hand, grew up attending the Salvation Army church in Canada, an evangelical Christian church. Her paternal grandfather was actually a church pastor. While going through a tough time during her freshman year following her first shoulder surgery, she was invited by a friend to a Fellowship of Christian Athletes service. During an altar call, she surrendered her life to Christ.

Though she had accepted Christ, she still attended parties, drank a little bit, and did some of the things she thought she needed to do to have that "college experience." When we first started going out, I observed her at a party and noticed that she didn't look comfortable in those surroundings. "It seems like you're trying to be somebody that you're not," I told her. I was concerned because she had told me all these things about her life in Christ, but I couldn't see it in her daily walk. She would later tell me that what I had said to her rocked her back into surrendering to God. Perhaps my questioning of her was my own way of coming to terms with my own estrangement from God. I was this egotistical guy from the golf team thinking that I was something special. In that way, we couldn't have been more perfect for or better for each other.

On our first date (my version) we talked about having a Christ-centered relationship, where we would uphold the tenets of the Bible in our everyday life. Yet as time progressed, we became sexually active for what would be the first six months of our relationship. But then Angie came to me and said if we were going to follow the Bible, we couldn't continue to have premarital sex. So we were celibate for the last two-plus years before we got married in 2004. We had this mutual yearning to grow closer to God and we were going to help each other through it in our relationship. "Let's grow our faith together and lean on each other," I told Angie. "Let's try to get better at this and challenge one another."

It was a progression. We didn't immediately begin following the Bible, but the seeds had been planted long ago and we had to give them water in order to give them life again.

I believe that everything in my relationship with Angie has worked for the good. For me, there has always been two roads. There is the shortcut and there is the long road, and somehow since Angie came into my life, I have taken the right path, even if it took longer. I have had many opportunities to go the wrong direction and I have made some bad decisions, but, luckily, I found my way back quickly. I am so thankful to God that Angie and I were able to put our faith in God front and center in our relationship almost from the very beginning.

About a year into our relationship, I gave Angie a promise ring with the blessing of her parents. In September 2004, three years after we met, we were married in a ceremony in Rome, Georgia, where she was an assistant basketball coach at Shorter College. At the wedding I cried so much that I almost couldn't get out the "yes" or "I do" during the ceremony. On December 26, 2004, three months after we were married, Angie and I were baptized together.

CHAPTER 7

Chasing the Professional Dream

At the end of my senior year at Georgia, I was still several academic credits shy of what I needed for graduation. So I knew that if I wanted to graduate, I would have to resume classes in the fall. But with the weather warming up and the summer golf season approaching, the next academic semester was the last thing on my mind. As usual, the first and only thing on my mind, besides when I was going to see Angie next, was how I would play as much high-quality golf as possible over the summer. My thoughts turned toward finally devoting myself to professional golf.

As I've mentioned before, in some ways golf is one of the easiest sports in which to turn professional. Basically, all you have to do is say, "I'm a professional golfer" and you *are* a professional golfer. This doesn't mean that you can play on the PGA Tour, but it means you can earn money playing golf. When people think about the game of golf, they often think in terms of money: the size of a purse in a tournament, a golfer's professional earnings over a year or career, sponsorship deals, and so forth. I always wanted to make money, but I was never especially motivated by it growing up. Our family had modest means, but I never felt as though I lacked a lot of things, so it wasn't as though I grew up dreaming of being able to buy lots of stuff. Maybe this owed to the fact that my parents took care of the financial side of life and made sacrifices so that I would be free to focus on golf, with the understanding that if I took care of golf, golf would take care of me.

Just how *well* golf would take care of me I couldn't fathom growing up and throughout college, but I never doubted for a minute that I would succeed at golf—that somehow, I would establish myself among the leaders of the sport. What motivated me was a passion to be always learning and improving so that, someday, I'd make the Tour.

But when you think about chasing your dream of playing professional golf, you inevitably focus on earnings because earnings are a very important measure of your progress in the game. With that in mind, I started playing in the mini tours, the entry-level competition for aspiring pros. Basically, the minis were a legal form of gambling where every player would pay a certain fee and then get to play for the pot. Cash prizes ranged from a few thousand dollars to as much as twenty thousand dollars for the top finishers, with a portion of the purse going to the company that organized the tournament. The early 2000s were a good time for the golf industry thanks to some guy named Tiger Woods. It seemed like there were a zillion mini tours around that summer, and I tried to play in as many as I could. Some were sponsored by local businesses, while others were sponsored by well-known companies. One mini tour I played early on, for example, was sponsored by Hooters and traveled all over the Southeast and up the East Coast.

In addition to the mini tours, which were open to anybody who could pay to play, aspiring golfers could try to earn a spot in what was called the Nationwide Tour. (Today, the Nationwide goes by the name of the Korn Ferry Tour.) The Nationwide was a developmental tour for the US-based PGA Tour and represented a step up from the mini tours. It included people like me who were trying to break into the PGA Tour as well as people who had already made the PGA Tour but failed to win enough points to stay in the top group. Here they could begin their assault back up the mountain. At the time, the top twenty winnings-earners in the Nationwide received automatic membership in the PGA Tour.

While the structure has been changed over the years, back then the paths to the Nationwide Tour and the PGA Tour were similar. You had to go through the Q School, which stands for Qualifying School. Q School is a series of tournaments that are held around the country every year. The tournaments are incredibly competitive—so competitive, in fact, that the majority of "professional" golfers who play in them never qualify for the PGA. They could still call themselves professional and make money, but they never moved up, even after trying multiple times.

To provide a sense of how competitive Q School was, in the typical years I participated in them, there could be anywhere from seven thousand to eleven thousand people who started out in the competition in dozens of places around the country. Through a series of local and regional events, that figure of eleven thousand would be whittled down to around one hundred fifty people who got to compete in the national final. Each one of those one hundred fifty participants was probably the best golfer anybody ever saw at his home course. When I was competing in Q School, the top tier of finishers at the national tournament got to play in the PGA Tour, while the second tier were invited to play in the Nationwide Tour. Either way, you were moving up in the world in terms of your status and your earnings potential.

Today, there is no direct route from Q School to the PGA's "big show." The top performers at Q School are given playing cards for the Korn Ferry Tour, named for the current major sponsor of what used to be the Nationwide.

I competed in my first Q School in 2001 and failed to qualify for anything. In 2002, I bested a pool of thousands of professional golfers to reach the national final, which earned me a spot on the Nationwide Tour. Once I made the Nationwide, I still competed in two more Q Schools, in 2003 and 2004, but didn't make it to the national final either year. My ticket to the PGA's big show would come about in a different way.

If this sounds confusing, welcome to golf, my friends. All I knew was that with a semester of college still left to finish, I had a long road to travel, so I decided not to waste any time and to try my hand at turning pro. I was still living at home with my parents that summer, so they put up the $400 or $500 entry fee for my first tournament, which was actually a Nationwide event held in Fort Smith, Arkansas. Since I hadn't earned my Nationwide Tour card yet—that came a year later—I had to qualify to play in Nationwide events. On top of the entry fee, we had to pay for a hotel room (my parents came with me) and food and gas, so the weekend cost to my parents was around $1,000. I won the qualifying round on Monday, which meant that I got to play in the Nationwide event the next day. I came in fortieth place and earned $2,500, which I offered to pay back to my parents. They told me I'd earned it and could keep it.

And that was my first paycheck as a professional golfer.

I spent the rest of the summer, as well as the rest of 2001, playing in the mini tours. My first months on mini tour were productive. After I began making money, I started paying my own entry fees, which usually ran between $200 and $500, and used my winnings to travel to more events and keep my equipment up to speed. After the Fort Smith event, I played in the Edwin Watts Pro-Am, a large tournament held at the Sandestin Resort in Miramar Beach. I wound up finishing fourth and earning another $4,500. But even more important, the owner of PING, John Solheim, happened to be attending the tournament since Edwin Watts was a big PING retail customer. This was the same John Solheim the local PING rep, Billy Weir, had written to about my 62 using PING clubs when I was twelve years old.

After the event was over, Mr. Solheim introduced himself and told me how much he'd enjoyed watching me play in the Pro-Am. Then he asked me whether I'd be interested in being "his pro." I'd been playing with PING clubs pretty much all my life and loved the brand, so of course I said yes. Soon after, I visited PING at their headquarters in Arizona. This began a relationship that has continued for my entire career and eventually led to me signing a lifetime deal with them at the end of 2020. But at the time I had no idea where the relationship would lead. I just knew that first deal provided a much-needed, short-term fix because as a PING professional I was able to get money that helped cover my entry fees and hotel bills, allowing me to focus on the golf.

I began winning or placing high on a regular basis and, for the first time in my life, started making money. I opened my first bank account. The number of people who competed in the mini tours determined the size of the pot. Generally, the summer tours were bigger and the prize money was better than the winter tour. From an earnings viewpoint, two of the largest purses I won were $15,000 and $22,000.

I'll never forget the Brewton, Alabama, event where I won

$15,000. The course was forty-five minutes away from my house. I had to pay $1,500 to play, and the winner got his money back times ten. I won the tournament by a few strokes and received one of those big cardboard cutout checks with the prize amount written across the front. It was the most money I'd ever earned, and it felt good to win that much money. But the truth was, I spent most of that weekend thinking about making the five-hour drive back to Athens to give Angie a promise ring I'd bought, and then taking a little vacation with her.

Before Angie and I left for a few days' rest, I met up with some friends who asked me how I'd done and what the prize was. When I told them, they went nuts: "Fifteen thousand dollars!" they said. That was a lot of rent checks, car payments, phone bills, and food bills. Fifteen thousand dollars was freedom to them! Since I was so focused on the dream, all I said to them was, "Let's go out to dinner. It's on me!"

When I was playing the mini tours, I developed a little system designed to give me the greatest possible exposure to competitive tournaments with the least amount of travel. Here's how it worked. Every Nationwide event included a Monday qualifying round from which a handful of people with the best scores would be invited to play in the Nationwide event. What I'd do is find places where Nationwide events and mini tour events were happening at the same time. On Monday, I'd play in the Monday qualifier. If I earned a spot in the Nationwide event, great. If not, I would play the mini tour.

In this way, I was playing in as many events as I could and getting lots of practice against all kinds of different players and all kinds of different golf courses. For me, getting better at golf and moving up the ladder was never about logging in lots of hours at the driving range. I grew up learning by playing and that's how I wanted to continue to grow as a professional. If I could make some money while learning, all the better.

Heath Slocum's dad, Jack, ran one of the better mini tours around at the time. It was referred to as the "DP Tour," which stood for Developmental Players. It held events all over, from the Florida Panhandle up into Georgia, Alabama, and Mississippi. I did well enough to win about half of the events and earn six figures a year. I know I said I wasn't motivated by money, but I didn't say I didn't like to buy things. After all, I was young, dumb, and had a love for cars. I remember during these years driving around Pensacola one evening with some friends and spotting this beautiful Mercedes CLK model drive by.

"Man, that's cool," I said. "I really want to drive a Mercedes just like that one."

"Why don't you buy one?" they asked.

"Nah, I can't buy one of those."

"Sure, you can. I'll bet you'd just love to ride that car to all your events," they razzed me.

I was still living with my parents, so I went home and asked my mom if she'd mind my buying the car. She told me that the money I earned was my money to do with as I saw fit, so my dad and I went to the dealership and bought a brand-new Mercedes. As we were getting ready to pull out of the dealership, I called Angie, who was back home in Canada rehabbing from a shoulder injury, and said, "Guess what I just did? I just wrote a check for $53,000 for a brand-new Mercedes CLK."

I expected to hear laughter or shouts of wonder, but what I heard instead was, "You what?"

"My dad and I are driving out of the Mercedes dealership right now," I told her.

"What Mercedes dealership?" she replied with a tone that told me she did not approve of my purchase, wherever the dealership was.

"Hey," I said, "I can buy a Mercedes if I want to. We're still just dating." I felt a little bummed out that she wasn't as excited as I was. A week earlier I'd flown up to Canada to visit her and meet her family for the first time. When talk turned to golf and my career, her dad asked me whether you could make money playing golf if you weren't on the PGA Tour. Most people don't understand the whole mini tour and Nationwide system. (Actually, a lot of golfers don't understand it either.) So I walked him through the whole process. But I'm guessing the Mercedes would have put his mind at ease. I mean, who goes out and buys an expensive car unless he has total confidence that he's going to succeed?

A couple days after buying the car, I drove it to Georgia to one of the DP tournaments and everybody was giving me a hard time about showing off and rubbing my success in their faces. I just said, "Man, I won a big tournament and went out and bought myself a cool car. Nothing wrong with that, is there?" And just to prove I knew what I was doing, I won that tournament, too, setting a course record on Saturday and breaking my own record the next day.

After three years of playing in the Nationwide Tour, I finally got my PGA Tour card. I wish I could say that I earned it by blowing away everybody in the country with my brilliance, but the truth was a bit more *nuanced*. The way it worked was that every year, the top twenty money-earners on the Nationwide Tour received an automatic place on the PGA Tour. At the end of 2005, I found myself in the twenty-first position in earnings.

Normally, this would have meant that I missed getting my tour card by a single place, which would have been extremely disappointing to say the least. But 2005 was not a normal year.

That year, Jason Gore won three times on the Nationwide Tour, earning an early promotion to the PGA Tour. He then went on to win a PGA Tour tournament, which meant he got a full PGA Tour membership on the spot. Because of his win on the PGA Tour, his standing on the Nationwide Tour money list was rendered null, and everybody shifted up one place, including me. That meant yours truly proudly received the twentieth and last PGA Tour card awarded for performance on the Nationwide Tour in 2005.

Getting my card opened up a whole new world for me. I could play in PGA tournaments and receive sponsorship endorsements well above anything I had gotten before. On the Nationwide Tour I was doing well financially and earned more than $200,000 in my last year there. Now I would be competing for much larger purses. In the back of my mind, I'd always imagined that I'd have a family, and making the PGA made me feel that I could support a family.

There are a couple of misconceptions about competing on the Tour. The first is that any player holding a PGA Tour card can automatically play in any tournament. In reality there are more players with PGA Tour cards than there are spots available in any single tournament. In other words, there's not enough room for everyone to be able to play every week. For this reason, players are grouped by priority levels, and new players often only get to play when some of the higher ranked players opt to skip a week. This means that lower ranked players do not control their schedule. Rather, they have to play whenever they can get into a tournament. The second misconception is that membership in the PGA Tour lasts forever. Once you earn your right to compete against the big boys, you have to earn your right to stay there. There are various ways to do this, including winning a PGA Tour event, which allows you to keep your Tour card for a minimum of two additional years. Another way to "keep your card" is by finishing in the top 125 of the season-long rankings. Fail to do one of those two, and you might end up with little or no status for the next season.

I knew that keeping my card was going to be no slam dunk. Every year, roughly half of the new PGA members fail to make the top 125 and have to drop back down to the Nationwide (now the Korn Ferry Tour). But I wasn't overly concerned about staying on the PGA Tour just then. I had my card and, even better, I had my first tournament: the Sony Open at the Waialae Country Club in Honolulu, Hawaii. One of my childhood heroes, Heath Slocum, would be there. So would Jim Furyk, Adam Scott, V.J. Singh, David Toms, and a bunch of other guys ranked among the world's top twenty players.

I'd be going toe-to-toe with big boys now. Things were certainly looking up.

CHAPTER 8

Playing with the Big Boys

When I was still playing on the Nationwide Tour, I earned a reputation as one of the biggest hitters in the game, as big or bigger than established professionals like Tiger Woods and John Daly. In 2005, my last year on the Nationwide Tour, I averaged 334 yards, some 18 yards longer than the next longest player. The golfing public was less familiar with the rest of my game, so at my first event since earning my PGA card, the Sony Open in Honolulu, I wanted to show myself and the world the complete Bubba Watson. None of us were disappointed.

During the Sony, I averaged 336 yards off the tee. On Sunday I even hit one drive that traveled a fairly ridiculous 398 yards. But I didn't just drive the ball long, I also went out of my way to "shape" a lot of shots around trees and doglegs, just as I'd done countless times back at Tanglewood and all the courses I'd played since then. Despite the attention the long drives received, it was my all-around game that earned me a fourth-place finish at my first PGA tournament. Sure, I was nervous playing my first event as a member of the PGA Tour, but for some reason it didn't bother me that week. I was on the PGA Tour, and I felt like I belonged.

After my success at the Sony, some in the media began portraying me as "the face" of a new breed of "bomb and gouge" golfers. As the name sounds, it was not always intended to be a complimentary phrase and was used to describe players who "bombed" the ball a long way off the tee into some rough and then "gouged" their way out of trouble. That's a pretty ugly description of golf, and it didn't suit me one bit. Much like big hitter Bryson DeChambeau and some others today, I had to listen to those eager to announce that this wasn't the way golf was supposed to be played.

These commentators left out an important point: at the Sony my putter was on fire, and six weeks after Sony I went down to Tucson and tied for third place, playing the event without a bogey yet somehow not winning, the first time in thirty years that had happened on the PGA Tour. Bomb and gouge? I don't think so. Overall, the attention was good for me because it helped introduce me to the golfing world, but it also began to open my eyes to the power of the media to create and shape stories about me (and anyone else). In the years to come, that would impact me in many ways, for better and worse.

Those two events in early 2006 got my rookie season off to a roaring start, but while I was playing well, I soon realized that I was going to have to turn my attention to a part of the game I hadn't taken seriously before: my caddie. I had made it from Bagdad, Florida, up through the mini tours without a professional caddie. On the mini tours and Nationwide when caddies were required, I took along a buddy from home. If the PGA Tour had said players could carry their own bags, I might have been first in line.

I thought that caddies were too focused on how much money they would be paid and getting raises if they stayed with me for an extended period of time. At that point in my life, I had carried my own bag 95 percent of my career. That was probably not the right way to think about it, but in that crazy head of mine I felt vulnerable, as though I was letting someone new into my world who might not understand me but was looking to make money off me. It sounds strange to say today, but I needed to wrap my head around the whole concept of caddies.

At the start of my rookie year, an older retired gentleman from back home worked for me as a caddie. He was trustworthy and very capable, but one day during my rookie season, he couldn't show up for work. And he had my clubs. The problem was, I had an 8:30 a.m. tee time in the third round of the prestigious Byron Nelson Tournament. I called the tour and told them that I needed to withdraw from the tournament. My club manufacturer could have gotten me another set of clubs, but probably not ahead of my tee time.

When Ben Crane, a fellow professional golfer, heard that I had withdrawn from the Byron Nelson, he invited me to come stay at his house, which was in the Dallas–Fort Worth area, so that I wouldn't have to travel back home to North Carolina and then turn right around and come back for the Colonial National Invitational Tournament, which was also in Texas. I was surprised by the generosity. I knew that Crane was a PGA Tour winner and a Christian, but I didn't know him well enough to expect that he would invite me to stay in his home. When I got in contact with my caddie, I told him to take two weeks off so that I could think about how to handle the situation. I replaced him with Josh Pape, another friend and golfing buddy from home, on an interim basis.

At Crane's house, Angie and I slept on a pull-out sofa during the week of the Colonial. It was during this time that Crane told me that I needed a real caddie who could help me play my best golf. I knew I was ready for a more serious caddie, but I also needed someone like me—focused on trying to become a better person. Crane told me he knew a caddie who fit my requirements. "I've got the perfect person for you," he said.

It wasn't an easy phone call to my old caddie and friend to tell him that I was replacing him with someone more experienced.

The world of tour caddies is a world unto itself. There are no ironclad contracts. Caddies can quit on players as easily as players can fire them. The caddies know the young guns coming up and how to get on their bags. They are looking for the next superstar. There wasn't much background on me. And no caddies were clamoring to work for me. One day, Crane got to talking with his own caddie who told him that there was one of those periodic "shifts" taking place when one caddie leaves a golfer, causing other caddies and players to make their own moves. When the name Ted Scott, better known as Teddy, came up, Crane thought he just might be the right fit for me.

Crane had gotten to know Teddy in the tour's weekly Bible study. At these Tuesday or Wednesday night gatherings, Crane was a vocal leader of this fellowship that had been meeting at tour stops since the late 1960s. Larry Moody was the tour's chaplain and leader of the Bible study. He used Scripture to help us keep in perspective everything that was happening on the golf course.

I was lucky to get Teddy after he was let go by Paul Azinger. During our first meeting, I'm afraid I didn't make the best impression on him. We met in the parking lot at the 2006 Deutsche Bank Championship outside Boston. Teddy was struck by how cold and distant I appeared in that first meeting—how I barely made eye contact with him. Just a year earlier, Teddy and I had a brief encounter in a PGA Tour course parking lot in Atlanta, where Teddy stopped me at TPC Sugarloaf and asked me to auto-graph an item for a charity.

Teddy once had his own aspirations to be a professional golfer. He fell into caddying in 2000 when the Buy.com Tour (also now the Korn Ferry Tour) came to Lafayette, Louisiana, where he was living. With a 102-degree fever, he had tried and failed on Monday to qualify for the tournament. So he showed up at the golf course the next day and asked if he could caddie. That tour stop was a place where many players still picked up local caddies for the week. Teddy hooked up with Grant Waite, a journeyman New Zealander, who had won the 1993 Kemper Open. Because of his fever, Teddy didn't start work until the first round of the tournament.

That first round was the first time he had ever seen Grant swing a club. On their first hole, Grant asked Teddy how far it was to clear a bunker. "It's a 2-iron," Teddy answered. "It might be a 2-iron for you," Grant replied. "But I don't know how far you hit a 2-iron. How far does it say in your yardage book to cover that bunker?"

"What do I need a yardage book for?" Teddy asked. "You're the pro."

Grant demanded that Teddy immediately get a yardage book, so Teddy sprinted back to the pro shop and brought one back to the course. It was 203 yards to cover the bunker, according to the yardage book. After all that back and forth and sending the caddie back to the pro shop, Grant chose a 2-iron to hit his shot. Teddy has been a professional caddie ever since.

Teddy has taught me the true value of a great caddie-player relationship. When I decided to hire Teddy, I made one request: please do not bring up money. It's not that I'm uncomfortable talking about money; it's just that I want my partnership with my caddie to be about golf and winning tournaments and not a running discussion about wages. My previous caddie had made it easy for me by asking me to pay him half of what most other tour caddies made. As a golf nut, it was a blast just for him to be out there around the best players in the world. I was spoiled by this arrangement, but I had a lot of years of carrying my own bag that made me less certain about the necessity of caddies.

After I finished twelfth in Boston and fourteenth the next week in Canada, Teddy told me that it was time to have that talk. "I don't want to be paid like a parking attendant," he said. "There is nothing wrong with that, but if you want me to be loyal to you, I want to be paid a little bit more. I am going to dedicate all my time and energy. In this relationship contract, you want me to go to battle for you in both golf and life and I want to be compensated for it."

Following that conversation, Teddy and I came to a financial agreement, and we've never talked about money again. He's earned raises and bonuses since establishing those terms and I hope he feels that I have paid him fairly, especially considering how often he's had to defend my character over the years, a job that he surely didn't sign up to perform.

I had told Crane that while I wanted a caddie who knew the game, it was more important to me that my caddie be at the same place I was in my life: a solid man of faith who loved his family and had a strength of character needed to do a difficult job. And being a caddie is a hard job. You have to be part sports psychologist, part mentor, and part friend. Over the years, I've learned that these roles can come into conflict with each other, and only a special person with a strong sense of doing the right thing can manage it.

Teddy is a rare person who combines all of the attributes you could ever want in a caddie. He was the first real caddie I ever had and, so far, he's been the only one I've ever had. A fifteen-plus-year relationship is fairly rare in professional golf. These relationships are like marriages. You have to maintain them. You have to have hard conversations, but you need to begin them from a place of love so that you can be truthful with one another and work through the problem. Otherwise, the problem won't go away. As players, we all get into a place where we can say some hurtful things to our caddies. This happens when we ourselves are in a place of hurt, of weakness or defeat. It takes a real man to be able to navigate through the good times and the difficult times and to hold the guy who strokes your paychecks accountable. Teddy and I would go through a lot of ups and downs together. I can't imagine ever having the career I've had without him.

During the next few years, Teddy and I got to know each other better and played a lot of golf together. From my rookie season in 2006 until 2010, I entered 106 PGA events and made the final cut for sixty-one of them. Of these, I managed thirteen top ten finishes and thirty-one top twenty-five finishes. I also managed to tie for fifth place in the 2007 US Open. This success began earning me more money than I'd ever dreamed of. I never really had to stress about staying in the top 125 and earning my Tour card for another year.

My reputation spread quickly during these years. Some of it had to do with my golf, and some of it had to do with my growing identity as some kind of homespun folk hero, an identity I encouraged whenever I could. I used to enjoy cutting it up with the media and would go out of my way to say things like, "When

I was born, my dad took one look at me and said, 'He's fat and ugly. Let's call him Bubba.'" Or, "I'm real lazy. I hate running. I just like to sleep. I heard Tiger and his caddie went out running yesterday. You won't see me or my caddie doing that." I referred to myself as a "new age redneck" because I didn't drink, hunt, or fish (although I have become an avid fisherman since). I even told one reporter that I'd quit golf before submitting to taking a lesson. "People say, 'Quiet your hips.' I don't have a clue what that means. I just hit it."

I liked to make people laugh and I wanted people to like me. But the truth was, I also wanted to stand out from the other golfers, not just as a golfer but as a person. When I started playing on the Tour, my equipment was PING but my driver shaft was made by a company called True Temper. The shaft is called a bi-matrix and it has graphite on the top of the shaft and about seven inches of steel at the bottom or tip. It is heavier than most driver shafts used today, but I have always preferred it because the strength of the steel reduces the torque, or twisting, of the shaft at impact. I've played my entire PGA Tour career with it even though few other professionals seem to use it.

When I turned pro, I did something with my club shaft that ended up defining me as a player. I asked True Temper if they would manufacture a hot pink shaft for my driver. Eventually, they agreed, and I began playing with it on the Tour. In later years, the pink shaft would become associated with cancer, but in the beginning all I really wanted to do was have fun and stand out. I even toyed with the idea of a green shaft, but I didn't like the way it looked, and nobody but True Temper would make a shaft with crazy colors, so I stuck with pink. It was my grownup version of wearing knickers when all the other kids wore jeans.

If I was the only one who did it, everyone would know who I was.

Golfers thrive not only by playing well and winning but also by building a personal "brand" that attracts fans and, along with the fans, sponsors. I was building a brand called Bubba from Bagdad, a brash, blue-collar guy who could do things with a golf club most people couldn't, but who most people could relate to. When you do this kind of stuff, you walk a fine line between looking like a goofball and looking like a goofball who can back up his attitude on the course. I thought I fell into the second category, somebody who liked to instill a little humor to defuse the tension but who also showed passion and respect for the game.

As far as my actual game went, Bubba the brand was attracting the attention of fans and professionals alike. Everyone seemed to agree I was a force, somebody whose long drives and ability to bully some of the obstacles that bothered other golfers was changing the way the game could be played. But gradually the public also began to wonder why I couldn't manage to close out tournaments and take home the trophy. I'd spent my developmental years trying to prove to everybody else that I belonged in the game; now I was beginning to feel as though I had to meet other people's expectations that I should be winning all the time. I wanted nothing more than to win my first event, since winning a PGA tournament would also ensure me two more years on tour.

Reporters were beginning to ask other players about me, and their comments also began to contribute to the legend of Bubba from Bagdad. Phil Mickelson, known as something of a power player himself, confessed that I was out of his league as far as my length was concerned. Some said I was inventing a new style of golf and coined the phrase "Bubba Golf" to describe the way in which I controlled the explosiveness of my swing by either cutting the shot or drawing it.

While I liked receiving attention, I thought that phrases like "bomb and gouge" and "Bubba Golf" kind of missed a larger point about how much fun it is to experiment with cool shots. Ever since I was a kid, I've enjoyed trying new ways of hitting golf balls. That's one of the reasons I don't practice at driving ranges: they are designed to encourage you to hit straight balls, one after the other. During practice rounds, I'd pretend that there were obstacles and hit around them. Then, when I'd play in actual games with real obstacles, I'd feel comfortable knowing that I'd seen it all before and had already figured it out.

It's an incredible feeling for me, but it does pose some challenges for Teddy. One of a caddie's jobs is to recommend clubs and shots to the golfer, based on what the caddie has learned about what the golfer can do with different clubs and drivers. Faced with the same distances or obstacles, most golfers will hit fairly predictable shots, the tried and true. But I would just as likely want to try something that nobody had seen before. So how's Teddy supposed to advise me on something he's never seen done or even thought possible? Sometimes, being Teddy has meant knowing when to go over to the cart and sit down and munch on some popcorn, because the chances are pretty good that if I think I can make a shot, I am usually right.

———

When I was coming of age in the late 1990s, my golfing hero was Tiger Woods. There had never been anyone like him: from the way he paid attention to all the parts of the game, to how he maintained his fitness and nutrition, to the incredible focus he had and his ability to beat guys mentally before they even stepped on the course. In February of 2006, I was playing at a PGA event at Torrey Pines in San Diego, and I knew Woods was playing at the same event. I told Teddy I wanted to see if I could play a practice round with him. Teddy said, "Okay, Tiger likes to get up early before everybody else to play his practice rounds. Let's plan to tee off at 6:30 a.m." The next morning, with barely enough light to see, we showed up, but there was no Woods. We waited a few minutes, and when he still didn't show up, we started our round.

When we got to the tenth hole, we passed near Woods, who, along with his caddie and a very large group of spectators for that early in the morning, was heading to the ninth. "Do you have room for me to join you?" Woods shouted to me. Being the knucklehead that I am, I looked around and pretended to confer with Teddy about it before saying, "Sure, Tiger, there's nobody here but me and Teddy." He smiled and headed over toward the tenth, leaving the spectators to look for a way to snake around the fairway and find their way to us.

Woods and his caddie came over, dropped the ball, hit one, and we just kept playing out the rest of the holes. After our round, Woods asked me whether I wanted to grab some dinner with our wives in the next couple of days. We traded cell phone numbers and enjoyed ourselves immensely.

Woods was used to people trying to line up practice rounds with him, so he was also used to turning people down. That same year, I started reaching out to Woods's people to see if I could get in some rounds with him and, to my delight, they agreed to set something up. We ended up playing half a dozen practice rounds over the coming months. Woods and I both liked to talk a little trash while we played, but try as I might, I couldn't help feeling especially energized every time I played with him. I felt like I wanted every shot to be pure.

To this day I am not 100 percent sure why Tiger agreed to play those practice rounds with me. I was a pretty young player at the time who had not won on tour, nor had I really done all that much to warrant the attention of an all-time great. At the same time, I believe Tiger is a true golf nerd. I have never met anyone who seems to love studying the game as much as Tiger, and to some degree I believe he saw my approach to the game as a bit of a novelty and it intrigued him. Not necessarily because of my length, but rather my tendency to curve the ball in the air so much more than everyone else. Many casual golf fans may not realize that Tiger is known for curing the ball both ways, too, just on a lesser scale.

So we played, and over the course of several rounds, Woods asked me some questions about my swing and how I approached certain shots and a lot of other things. The fact was, he did most of the asking and talking, not because I was in awe of him or didn't think I could learn from him but because I learn from watching, not talking. When I was younger, for example, I was watching Woods on television and found myself focusing on the way he brought his club head out to the right so that it looked like he was going to strike the ball over the top. I started making my swing go way out like his so I could cut it, and I started cutting the ball better.

I think my lack of questions may have bothered Woods, who may not have realized how much I learned from just being around him, but I chalked it up to different learning styles. He'd grown up with coaches and teachers and developed a highly verbal, interactive style of learning. I was a visual learner who never had coaches and learned more slowly. I wasn't used to lots of back-and-forth and quickly showing huge improvements. For me, learning involved slowly and steadily getting better. To use the analogy of travel, Woods was the kind of driver who would get on MapQuest or GPS and write down the directions for how to get somewhere and then memorize them. I would probably just drive east until I saw something that looked familiar and then try to figure it out. It's hard to say which method is better, but you are who you are, right?

The next year, Woods resisted my pestering about playing more practice rounds. I took it as an opportunity to prank him on it. "Oh, come on man," I'd say to him, "I know you're playing at so-and-so next week. I can help you get around that course." He laughed and then told me how crazy busy he was and so on. He knew I loved him to death and respected him 100 percent, and he was wise enough to know that our styles were simply too different.

Playing with the big boys was my lifelong goal, and Tiger Woods was the biggest of the big. Playing with him taught me that I could stand toe-to-toe with the world's best, which I felt I had done during those practice rounds. I began to realize that when I played my best, anything was possible. I also began to realize the true difference between Tiger and everyone else wasn't just the quality of his play but also his ability to consistently rise to the moment when his very best was needed. Having been on the Tour for a while, I also gained a strong appreciation for his uncanny ability to post a good score even when he wasn't playing his best. Rather than letting one bad round take him out of a tournament, he managed to salvage a good score for the day and rebound the next day. That was something I knew I had to get better at. One topic I wish I'd thought to ask him more questions about is the mental side of the game. When it came to playing for fun, I felt nobody in the world was better than me. But when it came to playing for serious stakes, with the world watching, I was a boy and Woods was a man.

Maybe if I'd asked him just a few questions about dealing with the stress of playing golf and living your life in the public eye, I could have saved myself years of bringing my negative thoughts under control. My dad raised me to be a leader, but being a leader didn't have to mean you couldn't ask for help. After all, there was no bigger leader on Planet Golf than Tiger Woods, and he knew when to ask for help.

One day in 2008 or so, Teddy and I got on the topic of my practice rounds with Woods. "Honestly, I don't think there was a single hole he outplayed you on," Teddy said. I know Teddy well enough to know he may have been boosting my ego a little bit, but his message was clear enough. Those practice rounds with Tiger helped me develop as a player. I may have been slow to apply some of the lessons learned, as per my usual style, but I have no doubt the experience helped lay the foundation for some of my success in later years.

In the middle of all of this, in 2007, Angie and I started talking about moving to Arizona. I was the one who initiated the conversation because I felt it was unfair to Angie for us to live fifteen minutes away from the family and friends I'd grown up with, while her family was in Canada. My family and Angie always got along well together, but when push came to shove my parents usually took my side. I had a wide circle of friends I played golf with or met for meals or just hung out with. Angie didn't have friends of her own. We didn't have kids, so we started playing golf together, and she started playing with some of the women we knew. When we weren't golfing together, Angie and I would watch movies, go out to dinner, go to church, play some games of one kind or the other, and just enjoy life.

Don't get me wrong. Life was good. But we felt something was missing, so we decided to move somewhere that was more "in between" our two families. We settled on Arizona because winters in the Pensacola area can be cold, and Arizona had a warmer climate and longer golf season. At that time, there was no year-round PGA Tour like there is today. The season ended for a few months and then started up again. So it was a no-brainer for us to be in Arizona during the winter.

We went to check it out for a couple of weeks. We visited the PING complex and I got to mess around with some clubs. We found a church that we loved and a golf course where I was allowed to practice. We fell in love with the place. One thing we weren't prepared for, however, were the Arizona prices. We weren't making a ton of money at that time and were looking at being asked to pay $100,000 for a golf membership. And even a small house that matched up with our Florida house would cost many hundreds of thousands of dollars.

We talked through all the details and decided that Arizona would help me with golf and help Angie make new friends who hadn't known me forever. We had a beautiful church to belong to where we would also meet new friends. And it would be better for both of us if we lived away from our families so we could grow as people and grow as a couple. It worked out tremendously well, and we got a taste for living in different places. Eventually, we bought a lake house in North Carolina near some friends so we wouldn't have to spend so much time flying back and forth between tournaments on the East Coast and West Coast. Once

October rolled around, North Carolina tended to get colder and there was less golf, so we'd move to Arizona and stay there until the next spring.

Ultimately, we would leave Arizona and move back to Florida, but we look back on those Arizona years fondly as a time when we got to spread our wings and become more independent as a couple. We now have a family vacation home in Arizona.

During this period, my growing stature as a golfer also led to my greater visibility in the media, which created a whole new and unforeseen set of pressures. Living your life in the public eye is difficult at best, but for me it was especially tough because I am not mentally and emotionally strong enough to just say, "Ah, forget it! What do they know!" Suddenly, I found myself constantly having to explain myself to everybody.

For example, in 2011, Angie and I decided to go to France to play in the Alstom Open de France, part of the European Tour. We couldn't wait to go, first because who doesn't want the opportunity to visit France, and second because Angie had played basketball there and we felt it was a special place for us. We were also invited to visit the facilities at Richard Mille, a sponsor, where they made intricate (and expensive) watches.

While in France, we had a blast taking Segway and bicycle tours around the city, visiting the Louvre and Triomphe de Arc, sightseeing, and eating all sorts of amazing food. At our hotel, our whole group befriended a professional tennis player from the women's tour and enjoyed forming a friendship with her and hitting the ball around. We even spent one afternoon visiting the Palace of Versailles.

As far as the golf went, I found the course very difficult to play. First, it was very windy, which would have affected the other golfers as much as me. Second, the European Tour has different rules for how they separate spectators and players: there are fewer ropes and, in some cases, no separation at all. Once, during a warmup round, Teddy and I were standing shoulder to shoulder going over a yardage book when a fan literally poked his head between our shoulders, smiled up at us, and began reading our book. During our actual play, spectators would wander onto the fairway while we teed off. Once, my playing partner couldn't find the tee box we were on and he ended up walking in front of me before my shot.

By now you probably know that I do not generally feel comfortable being around lots of people. Add the combination of the layout and the wind and it's not surprising I missed the cut after the second round. As I walked off the course, an interviewer asked me for my thoughts. What did I think of the tournament? What did I think of my visit to France? With a head full of negative thoughts from my frustrations on the golf course, I told him that I thought the tournament was "different" than the American Tour, with less crowd control and harder-to-find tee boxes. I didn't say I didn't like the tournament or the competition or France or anything else, only that it was different.

I went on to tell him how much we loved visiting France and that we planned to stay a few more days to relax even though I was out of the tournament and could have headed home. I mentioned that we'd gone sightseeing, and when the interviewer asked where, my real troubles began. I didn't know how to pronounce the French words, so in place of the Louvre I said, "The L Place"; in place of the Arc de Triomphe I said,

"The Arc Thing"; and instead of the Palace of Versailles I said, "The Castle of Versailles." (That last one wasn't entirely my fault because the little tourism pamphlet called our tour of the palace "The Castle Tour.") I wasn't making fun of the country. I wasn't making fun of the people. I wasn't making fun of anything.

Afterward, articles and social media posts began to come out calling me a typical "ugly American" who had embarrassed himself and his country. The more stories that came out, the more inventive were the falsehoods they reported. These included the claim that I had been paid six figures just to show up to the tournament, that I wouldn't let other players ride in the same car as me that took players from the hotel to the venue, and that I celebrated my loss by buying a $10,000 bottle of champagne and pouring it down the drain because I don't drink. Ironically these stories mostly ran in the US media, as the French media seemed to have no issue with my visit.

People called for me to return the advance money I'd supposedly received. They criticized me for wearing an expensive Mille watch instead of donating it to charity. Well, the truth was that I wasn't paid a dime to show. I came to do what I always do, and that was compete to win for prize money. I've definitely wasted ten grand before, but never on champagne. If I didn't share a car, it was because we needed room for my entire team, which included me, Angie, Teddy, my trainer, my manager, and a big bag of golf clubs. And by that time, I'd donated hundreds of thousands to charity and would give millions more down the road. So if I wanted to indulge myself and honor my sponsor by wearing an expensive watch made by that sponsor, well, that was my business.

What the media didn't choose to cover was how the people

of France welcomed me with open arms when I came back to the same venue as a player on the 2018 Ryder Cup team.

————————

When I was growing up, I used to love watching certain shows on television with my mom and dad. I liked shows like *Knight Rider, Airwolf,* and *The A-Team.* But my favorite was *The Dukes of Hazzard.* In 2012, I heard the iconic car they drove, the General Lee, was up for sale, so I went to Barrett Jackson Auction in Scottsdale to check it out. Since the car was expected to sell for several hundred thousand dollars, I didn't intend to buy it, but I wanted to make a bid, just so I could say I bid on the General Lee. The bidding got up to $100,000 pretty fast, at which point it just seemed to stop. Maybe that was a sign that I should have stayed out of it, but I had come there to make a bid and so make a bid I did—for $110,000. I waited for somebody else to bid. I turned to talk to somebody and, before I knew what was happening, I heard the hammer coming down loud and clear. Holy guacamole! I owned the General Lee. And not just *a* General Lee, but Lee #1. The very car that could be seen jumping in the opening credits of each episode.

The auction took place in Scottsdale shortly before the Phoenix Open, so for fun I drove it to the Phoenix Open. It almost always caused a sensation. Some people wanted to drive it. Who doesn't like a car that jumps? Other people just wanted to take pictures of it because like me they had grown up watching the TV show. After those first couple weeks, driving around in a 1969 Charger and climbing in and out through the windows like the characters on the show got a bit old, so the car was more or less retired to a garage for safekeeping. Like a stash of old baseball cards, knowing I owned the car made me happy because it reminded me of my youth.

Then, several years later in 2015, our country was rocked by a deadly shooting in South Carolina. That shooting instantly brought a renewed focus on the Confederate flag. Almost at once, it seemed that the entire world decided that the car I owned was inappropriate and racially insensitive. They said this because the car had a Confederate flag painted on its roof. My arguments that the car, and the family-oriented show that featured it, were about bootlegging, not race, weren't successful in changing the media's opinion of the car or me. With hindsight I can see their point. . . . I mean, who was going to believe a white golfer named Bubba from Bagdad? To the average person I was a walking billboard for the stereotypical redneck, right? Even if that wasn't who I was. After that period of intense focus on the Confederate flag, I never really felt the same about the car again. While I continued to own the car for several more years, it stayed in storage, only getting cranked from time to time to ensure it would still run. I had a lot of mixed emotions about what to do with the car. We talked to a few museums about donating the car but the ones that seemed to be a good fit often didn't want to deal with the potential controversy around the car. After a while I had the roof flag painted over. Even though the car never really saw daylight, for some reason it felt right.

Now, some critics will probably accuse me of defacing a classic, but the truth is, the paint wasn't original. The entire car had been restored and repainted a couple times long before I purchased it at the auction. Eventually a mutual friend connected me with a car collector out of Texas who was keen on obtaining the car for his personal collection. With mixed emotions I let it go. When I think about the car today, it no longer reminds me of some warm and distant time when I used to watch *The Dukes of Hazzard* with my parents. Instead, I think of the controversy that embroiled the car in recent years. In the end, I think that is why I finally let it go—its purpose, my reason for owning it, had come and gone.

CHAPTER 9

Tough Love from Teddy

"I love you to death, but I cannot keep doing this," Teddy was telling me. "It's just miserable out there. You're spinning your wheels, and we need to change this. I understand that you could fire me for telling you these things, but I have to do my job. You're living and dying over every shot."

After I failed to make it through the 2010 US Open sectional qualifier, Teddy and I sat down for an early dinner with my trainer, Andrew Fisher, at a Chipotle restaurant in Columbus, Ohio. I ordered my usual burrito with chicken, black beans, cheese, and brown rice. These post-tournament meetings were always about what we could do better as a team to prepare for the next event. It was nothing out of the ordinary when Teddy told me how much I was letting my mental game hurt my performance. But he had something else on his mind. A few days earlier during the Memorial Golf Tournament, I had embarrassed him with my temper tantrums on the course.

None of this really surprised me. Over the past several months, Angie had made similar comments. "Your Christ walk is not good on the golf course," she told me. "But it's good everywhere else."

Yet Angie was not my caddie, the person most responsible for helping me perform my job at a world-class level. No matter what, she would be there for me. Teddy, a fellow Christian, on-course therapist, and friend off the course, could take another job. I didn't want him to quit.

Life has always been pretty good for me off the golf course, but inside the ropes I can become a head case—a negative, self-absorbed, and self-defeating person in pursuit of unattainable perfection. No one has had to bear this burden more than Teddy. On tour, we spend a lot of time together. We share meals and, when Angie and the kids aren't traveling with me, I often will get him a hotel room next door to mine. Off the tour we take a break from each other and use that time to save up stories for back at work on the golf course. During the first year that he worked with me, in 2006, it was mostly all business. We were focused on learning how to work together. Caddies have to know their players. Teddy had to learn how far I hit the ball with each club, my energy level and mood swings, and what shots I could hit so that he could guide me in the right direction. He couldn't do his job well if he couldn't be honest with me.

It can only strengthen your relationship when a man who depends on you for his livelihood can come to you, look you in the eye, and tell you what you're doing wrong. I know a lot of players on tour who try to restrict their relationships with their caddies to the course, because they understand that this is a business; when you're playing bad, something has to change, and you can't fire yourself. I see Teddy as a friend who happens to also caddie for me. I've got to have a strong man of faith right beside me.

A day earlier, during the 2010 Memorial, several caddies complained to Teddy about my behavior. A couple of them called me a psycho and said that I was distracting their players when I was paired with them. *A psycho?* That's not what I wanted to be. I didn't want to be a distraction on the course. And I wasn't being kind to Teddy. Seemingly, I had no control over my behavior on the course. Later when other players began to complain about me to Teddy, he would tell them that if they had a problem with me they should speak to me personally. Teddy was tired of being a sounding board for their complaints.

———

The 2010 US Open sectional qualifier was the Monday after the Memorial. It is annually one of the most grueling days in golf—36 holes over two golf courses in one day—at sites all over the country. During the qualifier, I made my first hole-in-one on a par 3 at the Brookside Golf and Country Club. Teddy called it. He thought since the hole sat in a little bowl that let everything funnel down to the pin that I had a good chance of making it. There had been two players in the group in front of us who had nearly holed out their shots from the tee.

On the next hole, I made a triple bogey, which cost me any realistic chance of qualifying for our national championship. As you might expect, in keeping with the trend, I didn't handle the sudden change of fortune all that well. At this point Teddy thought I was losing my mind. He was struck by how I could act like a "psycho" on the course, but could be the nicest, most charming and relaxed guy off the course. He had no doubt that my lack of emotional control on the golf course was holding me back as a golfer, and it frustrated him that I didn't see it too.

Now, after putting him through five days of misery, I was seated at Chipotle laughing and cutting up with my trainer.

Teddy uses Scripture when he wants to make a strong point. This is a habit that comes from regular Bible study. Quoting 1 Thessalonians 5:11, Teddy told me that the Bible tells us to rebuke one another and encourage one another in Christ and that he was about to do both. Although I'm always paying attention, I'm usually busy playing on my phone or fiddling with something and not making much eye contact during these conversations. But I stopped everything and looked right into Teddy's eyes after he quoted from Paul's letter to the church of the Thessalonians. As I sat directly across from him at a high-top table, he told me that if I didn't change, he no longer wanted to work for me. "You're not being who you want to be," he told me. "You're not even trying."

With such a stern rebuke, Teddy believed he was about to lose his job. To him, I was a prideful know-it-all who wasn't open to learning or change, but what he didn't know fully was that I was, in fact, open to change. Teddy gets to see me at my most vulnerable place. I tell people that I'm a Christian, but you go play golf with me in a high-pressure situation, you might come back and say, "I don't want to be a Christian like that guy."

Sitting at that table, I promised Teddy I was going to work on being better.

———

After that conversation with Teddy at Chipotle, I didn't enter another PGA Tour event until three weeks later at the Travelers in Hartford. I spent a fair amount of those three weeks praying for discipline. It was easy for me to absorb Teddy's rebuke and encouragement to better myself, but I hadn't yet been tested under fire in a setting that brought out the very worst in me. That moment came halfway through the second round on the ninth

green at the TPC River Highlands. There I started to demon-
strate some of that childish petulance for which I had become
known around the Tour. Teddy walked up to me quietly, where
no one could hear him, and said, "Bubba, I don't know if you
remember what you said when we were at Chipotle, but the
clubhouse is right there. I'll walk in right now. Either change or
I'm going in. I'm not going to sit here and listen to this."

In the middle of a competitive round, it's not easy to turn on
or off your emotions. Moments of joy and disappointment come
and go. I had always tried to balance those contrasting feelings with
jokes and humor on the course, but when something went wrong, I
could have a nasty eruption. I collected myself enough to reset and
think about what I needed to do in order to both control my emotions and play good golf for the remainder of the week. In my first
four years on tour, I had become famous for my long drives and
pink shafts and misbehaving on the golf course. Becoming a celebrity before becoming a Tour winner invited scrutiny from fans and
the media. I had won consistently on the mini tours, but never in
three years on the Nationwide Tour. And with four second-place
finishes, I had been in contention and felt that Sunday afternoon
pressure. But victory still eluded me on the big Tour.

Unless your name is Tiger Woods, your goal is to always win
tournaments but to accept lesser outcomes, such as making cuts
and racking up top tens and twenties, the solid achievements that
add up to a good career. When I first got on tour, I was happy
just to be there amongst the greatest players in the world. In
professional golf you are an independent contractor with no job
security. If you play well, you get to retain your Tour card for
the next year. If you don't play well, you go back to the qualifying tournament or to the mini tours. I had comfortably stayed
inside of the top 125 in the FedEx Cup standings to keep my

card from year to year, but I had none of the security that came with winning.

Coming into the final round six shots back of the lead at the Travelers, I was realistically hoping for a top-ten finish. Justin Rose started the final round with a three-shot lead, but he struggled to a 4-over 75. My 66 got me into a playoff with Corey Pavin and Scott Verplank. This was the perfect opportunity to impress Pavin, who was the US team captain for the 2010 Ryder Cup. I wanted to make his team more than anything. I had always respected his shot making. I thought of myself as a juiced-up version of him. I saw that clearly on the first playoff hole when I hit my drive 320 yards and he popped up a 3-wood to just 220 yards. A fifteen-time Tour winner and the 1995 US Open champion, Pavin was in his first year on the Champions Tour and was playing at the Travelers primarily to scout players to fill his team for the Ryder Cup matches at Celtic Manor in Wales.

Too much of a competitor to simply go through the motions, Pavin had scrambled in his characteristic way to a 66 in the final round to get into the playoff. He was eliminated with a bogey on the first playoff hole, where Verplank and I both made birdies. On the second hole of the playoff, I beat Verplank with a par to earn my first PGA Tour win. I was relieved and happy to have the two-year exemption that came with the win. But that paled in comparison to what else it gave me: an opportunity to publicly thank Teddy, who had for four years endured my rants on the course.

It was made more emotional by what was happening in my personal life. My dad was battling terminal throat cancer and getting weaker every day. Angie also had a health scare. She was diagnosed with a tumor in her pituitary gland, and we were scheduling appointments with doctors to try to find some answers.

As I promised Teddy, I worked on being a better role model. But as is usually the case when someone is attempting a major shift in his action, I was inconsistent.

————

Later that summer I came very close to winning the PGA Championship, losing in a three-hole playoff to Martin Kaymer at Whistling Straits. Though I was in the heat of contention to win a major championship, my mind wandered to the Ryder Cup and to my father. When Kaymer won on the third playoff hole with a bogey after I had hit my approach into a greenside hazard, I was excited that I had secured my place on the Ryder Cup team. It was the honor of my life to play for my country.

My talks with Teddy, his stern but compassionate rebukes of my behavior, served as a constant reminder for me of both my responsibility to him and to God to walk in my faith on the course. But change can be a long and difficult road. After our talk in 2010, I generally did better for a couple years. But I still had some rough patches. One of those rough patches came in 2013, the year after I won my first Masters. I was back at one of my favorite tournaments, the Travelers Championship, with a chance to win late in the final round. At the par 4, 171-yard sixteenth hole at the TPC River Highlands, I was in between clubs and Teddy recommended I hit a 9-iron instead of the 8-iron I had in mind. When a gust of wind came up, my ball hit the bank fronting the green and rolled backward into the water. My first reaction was disbelief. "Water," I said as I walked off the tee toward the drop zone. "It's in the water. *That* club." After I took my penalty shot and hit my third shot onto the green, I turned to Teddy and asked, "You're telling me that's the yardage?"

I was still fuming when I missed my putt for double bogey. "There's just no reason for me to be here," I said, looking at Teddy. A gust of wind had come up and I didn't have enough club to clear a water hazard. This happens every day at all levels of the game, but with me being in contention, that shot going in the water along with my emotional reaction and comments to Teddy became the central story of the tournament. In my heart I feel I wasn't intending to blame Teddy, rather I was venting about the outcome of the shot.

Teddy and I disagree to some degree on what happened that afternoon at the Travelers in 2013. He believes that my anger and frustration were directed at him. It is easy to understand why he feels that way, and if you watch the video clip, it is not hard to appreciate his version of the day. All I can say is that, in the end, every decision is ultimately on the player. No one made me hit a 9-iron. I knew it then and I know it now. In the heat of the moment, I let my emotions get the best of me, and that was a mistake, but it was driven by frustration with myself because, once again, that decision was always on me. There was some lingering hurt for Teddy, I think, in the aftermath of the incident when the #PrayForTedScott hashtag was created and began trending on social media. What's certain is that there were many people around me who were whispering to Teddy about the way I was treating them and others since winning the 2012 Masters. In many ways I was worse off in 2013 than I had been in 2010 when I hadn't won a tournament. While I was still Bubba from Bagdad, my profile had risen sharply after winning the 2012 Masters and I was letting the superstar treatment get to my head.

By the end of 2013 I realized it was time for me to take responsibility for my own behavior. I needed to get away from believing that I held all the answers to my problems and that no one could help me. I started reading more and asking people questions. Heading into the 2014 season, I told myself that I was never going back to that dark place on the course.

CHAPTER 10

My Best Year and My Worst Year

In 2010, five major things happened: I told my father I loved him, my father died of throat cancer, Angie had her own health scare, I won my first PGA event, and I made the US Ryder Cup team. It was my best year . . . and also my worst.

Actually, a sixth thing happened, too, which was that Angie and I decided we would start the long and arduous process of starting a family through adoption. But that is a topic of its own chapter, so I won't dwell on it here.

The previous year, I was feeling pretty confident. I thought of myself as a cool dude who dressed cool and drove cool cars. I was ranked in the top 100 players in the world, but I thought of myself as on top of the world. Angie and I were also growing in our faith together, reading the Bible and asking questions, so I felt spiritually whole and good about myself. I wasn't happy with my performance in tournaments—I still hadn't won a PGA event—but I felt certain that I could turn that around.

Then one morning my dad called and told me he had throat cancer. I asked him how bad it was, and he replied that it was very bad. He probably had only a few months to live. At that moment, I felt a sense of panic and dread like I'd never felt before. Angie and I jumped on a red-eye flight and went down to see him. On the way down, Angie told me her head hurt. She said it felt different from a typical headache and was right smack in the middle of her forehead. I could tell it worried her. When we got to Pensacola, she wanted to check into the hospital. Angie's a professional athlete who had surgery on her knees, shoulder, and everywhere possible, so when she said she wanted to go to the hospital, I knew something was wrong.

After checking her in and taking some scans, the doctor informed us she had an enlarged pituitary gland.

Oh, that can't be good, we thought. But all the doctor did was warn us to come back immediately if Angie's vision started "closing in on her." In Pensacola, we spent a week or so with Randall and his wife and visited with my dad. I talked to Randall and some other people to find out where we could find the best expert on pituitary gland issues. It turned out that Duke University Medical Center had just the guy. So, in March of 2010, Angie and I met him at Duke.

After looking over the scans that had been sent over by our doctor in Pensacola, he said, "You're fine. No worries." And he walked out. Just like that. I thought, *Whoa, wait a minute*, and got him to come back in to give us a little more detail. He explained that nearly every woman over six feet tall has an enlarged pituitary gland. It wasn't a cause for alarm. The headache she had experienced during the flight and afterward might have been due to dehydration or fatigue. Nothing to worry about unless it happened again. We left Duke still feeling a little on edge but, overall, enormously relieved.

After visiting with my dad, Angie and I had gone back to Arizona for a while and I tried to busy myself with playing, but

Teddy knew something was not right with me. Although Angie was out of the woods, my father was worsening quickly. I found myself trying to turn my frustration at playing below my expectations into a positive passion to play for my family, especially my dad. When I flew off to play in an event, I knew he was sitting back there in Pensacola watching on the TV. I wanted to give him something fun to watch to ease his pain.

"Brother, you're hurtin' and something is going on. What is it?" Teddy asked. I told him I couldn't shake the chronic anxiety I felt knowing my rock and the person who taught me more than anybody else had was dying. Teddy figured as much and knew it would help if we talked. But talking about serious matters wasn't something my dad and I did. So Teddy said, "Your dad loves to read, right? He's, like, the biggest reader I know. He's even got a little library at home, right? So, let's write him a letter."

Well, my dad and I may not have liked serious talks, but I liked writing and reading even less. I told Teddy this, and his reply was classic Teddy: "Okay, *I'll* write the letter." I can't recall what was written exactly word for word, but it was about how I loved him and wanted him to be happy in heaven when his time came to go to the Lord. It told Dad how much I loved God and that I hoped he would get to know the Lord as well. It said that the Lord would always love him, and it was never too late to give your life to him.

After we sent the letter, I never asked my dad whether he read it, or even if he received it. I never brought it up directly with him. But one day when we were talking on the phone, he told me that when he got to heaven, he was going to become a great golfer so he could beat me.

"Dad, heaven ain't *that* good a place!" I told him.

Playing golf in heaven became our inside joke, the place we

went when things got too serious. For example, shortly after one conversation in which my dad told me he'd once scored a hole-in-one, and I had better work on getting one, too, I actually got my first ace trying to qualify for the 2010 US Open at Pebble Beach. I failed to qualify, but a couple weeks later I got another ace while playing with some friends at home. First thing I did was get on the phone and tell my dad he'd have to work hard up in heaven because I just got two holes-in-one.

Talking about golf was the way I could communicate with him about heaven.

I knew my dad would be glued to the television for the 2010 Travelers Championship at TPC River Highlands in Connecticut. I made the cut, played pretty well, and on Sunday started six behind Justin Rose, who held a three-shot lead after 54 holes. Rose could have won by shooting a mere 1-over 71, but he stumbled a bit and fell to a 75, tying for ninth place. His playing partner, Ben Curtis, went from being tied with Rose on the twelfth tee to finishing tied for thirteenth. I was headed in the opposite direction and shot a 66 to tie for the lead with Corey Pavin and Scott Verplank. At the time, Pavin was fifty years old and serving as the US Ryder Cup captain. He was taking a break from the Champions Tour to scout players for the 2010 team.

The playoff began on the 444-yard eighteenth hole at TPC River Highlands. Both Verplank and I hit our tee shots much farther than Pavin. Mine went 320 yards. I'm not sure how far Verplank's went, but Pavin missed his tee shot, leaving him some 100 yards behind me and leading him to lose the hole. "The playoff was a little disappointing to me," Pavin said afterward. "Now it's just time to go back and play with golfers my own age."

That left Verplank and me to play the sixteenth hole. After I won it and my PGA event, I began to cry. "You know, I've never had a lesson," I told the person who interviewed me. "My dad, he took me on the golf course when I was six years old and just told me he was going to be in the woods looking for his ball, so he just told me to take this 9-iron and beat it down the fairway. And now look at me after beating a 9-iron on the fairway, coming from Bagdad, Florida. I never dreamed this."

And then I told them the real reason I wanted to win the Travelers. "I wanted to win it for my dad who is dying of throat cancer. I love you, Dad." That was the first time I publicly shared what had been going on with my dad. Later on, I would also say that I wanted to impress Corey Pavin so I could make the Ryder Cup team. "But that's a whole different story, Corey, if you're listening."

For many people, seeing me cry and hearing me profess my love for my dying father on television may not have seemed that strange under the circumstances. To appreciate the significance of that moment, you have to understand some of the events leading up to the Travelers tournament. Not long before the tournament, I had flown down to Pensacola to visit my dad. When I got there, he was sitting on the porch. We talked a little bit about golf and what the doctors were telling him. And then I got in my rental car to drive away. I got about a few hundred yards down the road when I decided to turn back and say something that needed to be said to my dad's face. I went up to the porch and told my dad I loved him. That was the first time either of us had voiced the words "I love you." I was crying and he was holding back his own tears, but he told me he loved me too.

After the initial interview on the sixteenth hole, where I'd sealed the playoff win, Teddy and I had to drive a cart back up to the eighteenth green for the official trophy presentation, and I was crying. Here, once more, Teddy asserted himself. He was happy for the win but thought I was spiraling a little bit out of control. He said, "Look . . ." Teddy often started his serious talks with me by saying "Look." "Look, Bubba, I know you're going through some tough times, but, man, you've got to pull yourself together. Nobody lives forever, you're going to have to go on with *your* life," he said.

Most people avoid talking about family deaths, but Teddy did me a great kindness by talking about my family. It occurred to me that this conversation was the very reason I wanted a caddie like Teddy, somebody who was grounded enough in Christ to share our lives and sorrows and joys when most others would be afraid to.

———

The Ryder Cup means so much to me and my family because that was my last event my dad saw me play in 2010. Somehow, I had managed to qualify for the team, first by winning the Travelers (at US Captain Pavin's expense) and coming in second place at the PGA Championship after losing in a playoff. Overall, the results moved me from eighteenth in points to third, earning an automatic spot on the team. A few minutes after the PGA playoff ended, I agreed to be interviewed on an XM radio spot that catered to sports, but I still wasn't 100 percent sure I'd made the team, so when the host launched into all sorts of random questions, standing there a few steps from the last playoff hole, I asked him if he'd heard any announcements about who made the Ryder Cup team yet. He heard my question but seemed to ignore it. So I told him that I was not going to answer any questions until we confirmed if I had made the team. I sat there and watched them scrambling with headsets, trying to go to commercial or whatever, and then, finally, after a minute of dead air, they told me and their listeners I was guaranteed a spot.

"So . . . how does it feel to have lost the PGA?" they followed up. "Not concerned at all," I deadpanned. "I'm all about the Ryder Cup!"

At the Ryder Cup in Celtic Manor, Wales, I was paired with Jeff Overton, also a Cup rookie, in the four-ball and foursomes. In session one of the matches, Overton and I beat Luke Donald and Pádraig Harrington three and two in the four-balls. This was considered an upset. Harrington was a three-time major champion and a veteran of five previous Ryder Cups. And Donald was on the brink of becoming the number-one ranked player in the world. Yet that would be the only point I would earn for the US team, as we would lose the Cup to the Europeans fourteen and a half to thirteen and a half.

I love the Ryder Cup because it's the best chance I have to honor my dad and serve my country, not exactly like he did but in the same spirit of pride. For me, playing in the Cup wasn't about hating on Europe or winning at all costs or that sort of thing. I wanted to win as much as anybody else because that's what competition is all about. But on any given day at any given tournament, some guys were going to play better than others. The individual or the team that played better one year might play worse the next. Besides, the Europeans we were supposed to hate during the Cup were a lot of the same guys we played day in and day out in the Tour. A lot of us were close friends.

I always thought the better way to look at the Ryder Cup was to see it as evidence of how much Americans have helped to grow the game of golf, and to use the event to continue to inspire more young people to play. If we want the Cup to inspire future golfers, let's keep it fun and exciting and not get so focused on not losing that we change the way we choose players or how we pick captains and how we eat and how we drink and so on. The idea of using the Cup to talk about "the state of golf in America" was invented by the media. It's not what golfers think about when they think about playing for their country.

———

Two months before he died in 2010, Dad and I participated in a golf outing for the Green Beret Foundation at the Naval Air Station course in Pensacola. The event gave me a chance to honor him. He was too frail and weak to walk so he rode in a cart. His T-shirt and jeans hung loosely on his then 100-pound frame. He fought back tears as he was presented a plaque honoring his military service. "It's great to see my old unit noticed by everybody again," he said, even though the plaque specifically called him out.

When he died, I announced the news on my Twitter feed. "Everyone, it's a sad day for my family! My dad has passed." A few hours later I wrote: "My dad got to see me win and play for the USA in the Ryder Cup!!! God's plan is always right! God gave my family my best year and worst year."

Today, when I look back to my dad's death, I feel a son's regret that he couldn't live long enough to enjoy more of the successes I would have and that he would have shared in. It would have given me more time to prove myself to him, although I suppose I'm still doing that today. But I also feel a father's wonder at the mystery of life. I mean, did that man ever think that his overactive and not overly bright six-year-old would grow up to win professional golf matches and donate millions to the Children's Hospital in Pensacola where he was born? If you'd have gone up to him while he was leaning against a tree with a beer in one hand and a cigarette in the other and said, "Gerry, your kid is going to grow up and quit baseball to play golf, and someday he will win two Masters tournaments without taking lessons and own part of an AA baseball team and a car dealership," my dad would have laughed.

"Sure," he'd have said. "But I'll be more than good if he does *half* of that."

CHAPTER 11

Our First Adoption

On the evening of March 19, 2012, while I was playing in the Arnold Palmer Invitational, Angie and I received a frustrating phone call from a California adoption agency telling us that a birth mother had chosen another family to adopt her child. We had experienced this disappointment before. There had been a child who we thought we might adopt. It had been a year-long process of traveling to meet the child and birth mother. We got to the point where we thought we were going to get the baby boy, so we took a picture with him and put it on display in our house. But the birth mother eventually selected a couple that lived within a half hour of her home. This last episode came down again to the same scenario—the birth mother picked a family from a state closer to where she lived.

We didn't want people to know that we were trying to adopt. Perhaps it was immature on our part to not want to talk about it with our family and friends. But it was never easy going through the emotions and then having another family tell us no. These women, often single mothers, had every right to choose whom they wanted to raise their children, but that didn't lessen our feelings of rejection.

What do you say when your crying wife looks at you and says, "Am I not fit to be a mom? I can't biologically have a baby and they are not even letting me adopt a child?" Angie had not been around a lot of babies, but when she was around them, she looked uncomfortable or nervous. She was scared to death of being a mom and now all these negative thoughts swirled in her head. She was placing blame on herself for us not getting the child because she took it as rejection of her as a woman by the birth mother. Perhaps if it had been the birth father making the final decision, I might have felt a similar kind of rejection. Yet I never felt a stigma or less than a man for not having biological children. Two of my closest childhood golf buddies, Robin Cook and her brother, Ryan, were adopted by Hiram Cook and his wife, Bonnie, who were like second parents to me.

Angie and I weren't prepared for the legal and procedural aspects of the adoption journey. We thought that people would look at our profile and see that we were two relatively financially secure athletes. Perhaps it was arrogant, but we never thought we would experience this kind of disappointment.

As a man, you don't know how to answer these questions for your wife. I didn't know what to say. I couldn't assure her that we were going to get a baby. We had always thought that we would be a couple that had kids and now we were doubting if that would ever happen. I just looked at her on that Monday night and told her how much I loved her. They were the most comforting words I could offer that I knew were true.

Angie told me that she couldn't have biological children on our first date. I was dropping her off after dinner when we fell into a long conversation sitting in my car outside of her apartment in Athens. Children were the furthest thing from Angie's mind. Her heart was set on earning an Olympic medal for her native Canada and getting a WNBA contract. One of her nicknames was The White Girl Who Could Jump. She was a gritty player who played good defense and got rebounds. There had been only one serious boyfriend in her life to that point and she had never had a real conversation with him about having children. When she shared with me that she couldn't have children, she had no idea how I would react. Without missing a beat, I told her that we could adopt. It was presumptuous on my part to think on the first date that I would have children with her, but I didn't want that issue to be a hindrance in our relationship.

After dating for a couple of years, we got married in 2004. She was coaching basketball at Shorter University, a small college in Rome, Georgia, and I was playing a combination of the Nationwide Tour and mini tours around the southeastern part of the United States. Within a year of getting married, Angie and I met with fertility specialists to discuss the possibility of her having biological children. They told us that her uterus was too small, which would have made it difficult for a baby to grow to full term. One specialist told us that if Angie got pregnant it would be a risk to both her health and the child's.

Neither of us looked at her infertility as a huge disappointment. For us, the choice of adoption became the ultimate public expression of our faith because it is one of the most profound works to describe what Christ did for us on the cross. We haven't done anything to deserve the salvation that we inherit through Christ's sacrifice. Through adoption, the lives of so many children are changed, which is the exact same picture of what Christ did. We had our faith and our convictions about adoption, but we didn't have a full grasp of the difficulty of adopting a child.

After living in Pensacola for the first couple years of our marriage, we moved in 2008 to Scottsdale, Arizona, where we eventually started the adoption process with a home study, which is where a social worker prepares a document detailing our values, personal feelings, and overall readiness for childrearing. I don't think that I have done any project in college that was as hard and in-depth as our home study. We had a really hard time getting through the paperwork because so much was required. It was also during this period that my dad was diagnosed with terminal throat cancer, and that didn't make it any easier to sit down and answer some of those questions about our upbringings. There were so many questions about my dad in the home study that, emotionally, I didn't want to think about. I was also working very hard to establish myself on the PGA Tour. So instead of the two months that it normally takes to complete a home study, it took us close to two years. It was shortly after my dad's death in the winter of 2010 that we began hearing from birth mothers about being chosen to match with a child for adoption.

On the Tuesday during the Arnold Palmer Invitational—the day after we had received the most recent bad news about an adoption—we received a phone call from an adoption agency that told us we had been chosen to receive a child as long as we said yes. They told us that we needed to get the child, who was in Florida, right away and that we couldn't take him out of the state until the adoption was final, a process that could take between three months and a year. Staying in Florida wasn't a problem; in fact, we had already been looking for a house in Isleworth, an exclusive gated golf community in Florida that has been home to many professional golfers. The problem was that up until then we had only been looking. We had not actually found a house, and in five days we would need to get this child and have a place in Florida to bring him home to.

We notified the agency on Wednesday morning that we were a definite yes. I skipped the Bay Hill Pro-Am, and Angie and I set out to find a place to call home. Since I wanted a house on the water, we took a house tour on a boat inside the Isleworth community with a real estate agent named Mark Hayes and the boat's owner. Mark worked for the real estate agency that sold nearly all of the property inside Isleworth. As we were taking the tour, Angie was texting back and forth with the adoption agency. "We have a dilemma," I said to Mark. "I need a house now."

"Why?" he responded.

We didn't want two men whom we didn't know to be the first people we told that we were adopting a child, but the reality of the situation was that they needed to know what was going on in order to understand our urgency and help us.

Trying to hedge my bets, I said, "Hey, can't we rent one if we don't want to buy now?"

At that point I explained that we wanted to adopt but that we needed a furnished house by Monday. Unfazed, Mark said he could help. It turned out that there were some homes on the property available to rent. We leased a house off the first hole at Isleworth without even knowing the cost. "We'll work it all out," Mark told me. "This is something way beyond a real estate deal. This is about helping someone." What I didn't know at the time was that the house had not actually been available for rent, but it was owned by a company related to Isleworth and Mark simply made it happen on short notice. He also made some calls and helped work it so that I could have playing privileges at the golf club. Our lives were changing forever at this moment. Angie was trying not to tear up and I was being the stoic tough guy.

The Bay Hill tournament was starting the next day and I didn't want to withdraw. I was playing well and coming off a second-place finish at the WGC-Cadillac Championship at Doral, where I had the lead going into the final round before stumbling on the last day with a 2-over-par 74 to lose by a shot to Justin Rose. We had all the details for how we were to receive the baby on Monday. A woman from the California adoption agency would fly in and take the baby boy from the birth mother and take care of the baby until we could claim the child. As excited as we were, Angie was saying that we had to keep the news quiet and not tell anyone in case something happened and the adoption fell through. On Wednesday night we celebrated and the next day I shot a 3-under 69 during the first round at Bay Hill. When Angie picked me up from the course after that round, our car was loaded with baby stuff. "You can't pick me up with a car full of baby stuff if you're trying to keep it secret," I said with a big smile. On Friday, I had a 70 and two even-par rounds over the weekend for a fourth-place finish.

On Monday, Angie and I drove to Fort Lauderdale to meet the birth mother, the one-month-old baby, the adoption agency manager, and a lawyer. We met them for lunch at a restaurant. I tried not to cry as the birth mother told us why she was giving up her baby son. There were two older children and another mouth to feed would be too much for her to handle. This woman didn't know that I was a famous golfer. She just knew that I was about to take her baby.

The birth mother asked if we were going to change the baby's name. "His name is Caleb," she said. Angie just started bawling when she said that. I told the birth mother that in honor of her we would not change his name. "Well, the reason why I named him that is because I don't know anything about the Bible," the mother said. "But somebody told me it was a great story."

Even though I call myself a Christian, I had never read the story of Caleb, who was sent by Moses to spy on the situation in the land of Canaan. When all the other spies said that Canaan was too powerful to be conquered, only Caleb and Joshua believed that it could be taken. God punished all the Israelites for their lack of faith in him, except Joshua and Caleb. Numbers 14:24 says, "Because my servant Caleb has a different spirit and follows me wholeheartedly, I will bring him into the land he went to, and his descendants will inherit it." We were all crying as we stared into the face of this little bundle of joy that we would forever call Caleb. Angie said that we would change his middle name from Lee to James. Angie was already calling him C. J. in her head, but that never stuck.

We had settled on the name Caleb James, but he still wasn't our child to take home. From the restaurant we set out in our separate cars for the lawyer's office. For about twenty minutes, the birth mother had some private moments with Caleb and said her last goodbyes. When she was done, she handed him over to us, his new parents. There is a photo of me and Angie from that day with Caleb in our arms. Angie is giving him a bottle for the first time.

Instead of nine months to prepare for a baby, Angie and I had just a couple of days. Her mother flew from Canada to meet us in Fort Lauderdale. We got a hotel room and sat down, as many new parents do, and simply stared at our baby. When Caleb started crying, we had our first panic attack about how to get him to settle down. The next morning, I flew to Arizona to tie up some loose ends with the adoption attorney, pick up some things from our house, and sleep peacefully in my own bed. I was back on a plane to Orlando on Wednesday. Angie had driven with her mom and the baby back to Orlando to the rental house. Her dad and my mom also came for a visit. By law, we wouldn't be able to leave the state of Florida with Caleb until the court gave us approval, and we didn't know how long that would take. Typically, the grandparents are competing to see who can do the most for the new baby, but not my mom and father-in-law. They announced that they were going with me to the Masters.

The Friday before the start of Masters week, the three of us set out for Augusta so that I could get acclimated to the conditions at Augusta National and to get my mind focused on playing a major championship. It was Angie who insisted that I leave a day early because she knew how well I was playing. She told me to go and focus on golf. I practiced on Saturday and told Teddy to just get there when he could. We had released an announcement about the adoption earlier because we wanted to be able to answer why Angie wasn't at the tournament, especially if I was in contention. It would look weird if the woman who was at my side at most tournaments wasn't there for the biggest event of the year.

Because I was one of the hottest players on tour, I started doing interviews at the beginning of tournament week under the big oak tree behind the Augusta National clubhouse. Most of the conversations were about Caleb. I admitted that I wasn't having much fun and that I was ready for the tournament to end so that I could get back home to be with him and Angie. Every day after practice I would rush into the locker room so that I could check my phone to see what new photos and videos of Caleb Angie had sent me. Every time that week that I played well and came in for interviews, it gave me an opportunity to tell the world how proud I was of my new son and how excited Angie and I were to be parents. I never even envisioned winning the Masters. I was so focused on playing golf. It was my moment to take a deep breath because my real life was going to happen when I got home. I couldn't wait to be with my wife in what was the happiest time of our lives.

Caleb's adoption would not be final for another six months. Since Caleb was a Florida resident and we lived in Arizona, we had to meet adoption laws in both states, which meant a lot of additional legal paperwork and extra meetings with our attorney. That May, we heard some criticism of my choice to pull out of the Players Championship, but I needed the break to handle my affairs and spend time with Angie and Caleb.

I never saw the boat driver again, but I did see the real estate agent, Mark, around Isleworth quite often. After a few months we were allowed to return to Arizona with Caleb, but we made our way back to Isleworth the following year after purchasing and renovating a home. Looking back, I am amazed how everything surrounding Caleb's adoption fell into place. I am eternally grateful it worked out the way it did.

CHAPTER 12

The First Green Jacket

At the Augusta National Golf Club, I was surrounded by a small group of reporters underneath the big oak tree behind the clubhouse. It was Saturday afternoon of the 2012 Masters and I had just finished my third round with a 2-under-par 70. Through 54 holes I was 6-under, three shots behind leader Peter Hanson and two shots behind Phil Mickelson, who with a win on Sunday would claim his fourth green jacket. This was my fourth appearance in the Masters, with a twentieth-place finish as my best showing in 2008.

As a twelve-year-old I had made putts on the practice green at Tanglewood while dreaming each shot was going to allow me to win the Masters. For years I had contended in the Future Masters, a prestigious junior tournament in Alabama.

But now a reporter was standing there asking me if I thought I could win the real tournament. "My goal is to get a top-ten," I said. "I'm just going to go out and play my game."

For dinner I had a burrito for the seventh night in a row. Before I went to bed I talked to Angie and looked at pictures and videos of Caleb that she had sent me. I awoke on Easter

Sunday, the seventeenth time that the Masters fell on the day when we Christians celebrate the risen Savior, Jesus Christ. It was a clear and sunny day in Augusta. For the final round, I was paired with Louis Oosthuizen, who had won the 2010 British Open Championship.

We went off at 2:30 p.m. in the second-to-last group. At the first hole, I dropped a shot with a 3-putt. We could hear the roar from the patrons on other holes, which was a sign of low scores being posted by players in front of us. Opening with a bogey wasn't at all what I needed, and Teddy didn't want me to get in my own head. He assured me that there was a lot of golf in front of us. We knew that Bo Van Pelt had come in early with a 64. The second hole at Augusta is a par 5 that is reachable in two. I made birdie there to regain the shot I lost back at the first and was back to 6-under-par for the tournament. Meanwhile, Oosthuizen hit his second shot from the fairway 260 yards into the hole for a double eagle, which vaulted him into the lead. I was so excited for Louis. The roars seemed to go on forever. I was envious of him because I had received a piece of crystal from the club every year that I had played in the tournament for making an eagle, but I hadn't registered one this week.

At the Masters the scoreboards are an integral part of the drama that occurs on a Sunday afternoon in a final round. Both the players and the patrons seem to hold their breath with every turn of these little windows that show the changes on the leaderboard. By the third hole, I saw a scoreboard that revealed that Louis was in the lead at 10-under-par and that I was four shots back of him. I told myself to keep grinding and that if I held it together, I could get a top-ten finish and possibly a top-five. After making a birdie at the seventh hole, I made six straight pars. At the short par-3 twelfth hole, I couldn't get up and down after missing the green and made bogey. I was now two strokes back of Louis and needed to give myself another pep talk. I was still in a good position, with good birdie chances at the two par-fives, the thirteenth and fifteenth holes. Since going 1-over on these two holes on Thursday, I had birdied each during the ensuing two rounds. I was excited because if I could make a couple of birdies, I could finish in the top five, make a boatload of money, then go home and have fun with Angie and Caleb.

After making a birdie at the thirteenth, I started to envision historic shots that I had seen watching the Masters on TV. I'm not a golf history buff, but I can remember certain shots and pin placements. I told Teddy that I wanted to hit this shot that Tiger had once pulled off at the fourteenth hole. Augusta National is a second-shot golf course, which means the real key to winning there is how you hit the second shot on each hole. At the fourteenth hole—the course's only hole without a bunker—the green is very nuanced. The green falls down the ridge from left to right, which forces the player to aim left of the target on the approach shot. For the traditional Sunday pin position—in the middle tier of the green—I needed to aim left and hope it came off the slope and funneled toward the hole. I had seen Tiger do it. From the short rough, I hit a 56-degree wedge that spun back off the slope and stopped six feet short of the hole. I turned to Teddy and said, "We did it!" I made the birdie putt. Although I was just a shot off Louis's lead, I still wasn't thinking I had a chance to win.

At the par-5 fifteenth hole, I hit a drive and made a two-putt birdie, but it still hadn't crossed my mind that I could win. I was so focused on trying to finish in the top five or top ten. I was also disappointed that I didn't make an eagle at the fifteenth. At the par-3 sixteenth, I hit a perfect 8-iron to within twelve feet of the hole. I remember thinking that if I made that putt, I would be in a tie for the lead. In my head I wasn't thinking about anything other than being in a tie for the lead. It wasn't about having a chance to win. When I made the putt for my fourth consecutive birdie, I was now tied with Louis for the lead at the Masters. On the seventeenth tee I said to Teddy—for the first time that entire day—that we had a chance to win the Masters. He said, "I know, man." Then he shut up so as not to jinx anything. The gravity of the moment finally had hit us.

———————

On the seventeenth tee, I sliced my drive left into the trees. Walking off that tee I said to Teddy that I might have ruined with that shot my second chance at winning a major. In 2010, I had lost in a playoff to Martin Kaymer at the PGA Championship at Whistling Straits. In the three-hole aggregate playoff, I took an early lead with a birdie on the first hole. After Kaymer birdied the second hole of the playoff, we went into the last hole tied. On the eighteenth hole, the third hole of the playoff, I was too aggressive from the deep rough and found the water hazard fronting the green. Kaymer played conservatively and his bogey ended up being good enough to win the championship.

That memory was racing through my head—these are the dangerous moments for a guy like me—as I walked down the seventeenth hole to my ball. "Don't even focus on that," Teddy told me. "Who knows what we got right now." When we got to the ball, it was one of the hardest shots I'd ever seen. The ball had rested on a moist piece of trampled-down grass that the patrons had been walking over all week. I had 155 yards to the hole, and I needed to hit a gap wedge up over the trees with this muddy lie and somehow hit it farther than I've ever hit it before. I gave it all I had.

The shot ended up in the middle of the green. Now thoughts of winning were creeping into my head. Louis had hit a tree with his drive, leaving himself a long approach shot that ended up in the front bunker. But he played a beautiful shot to the green. We both made par and headed to the eighteenth hole tied for the lead. All I could think was, *Well, wow!*

Walking to the tee I said to Teddy, "I'm going to live and die by my driver. So I'm hitting driver here. No playing safe. We're going to go after it." I hit it right where I needed to, so I twirled my club and picked up my tee really fast. My heart was racing . . . it felt like the patrons might be able to see it pounding right through my shirt. Still, I was trying to look cool. Louis also hit a great drive. In the fairway, he hit his approach shot long and had a lengthy birdie putt. I hit my second shot to about fifteen feet. It was a putt that I'd seen players make and win tournaments, but I missed it. Louis and I would leave that eighteenth green tied for the lead and headed for a sudden-death playoff.

As I walked through a corridor of what seemed like thousands of patrons to sign my scorecard, I tried to keep my head down and stay focused. Phil and Peter Hanson had to play eighteen, and if Phil holed his second shot out of the fairway, he could tie us for the lead. When he didn't, the playoff was set. The Masters has a playoff format that begins at the eighteenth hole and if a champion is not determined there, it goes to the tenth hole, alternating between those holes until a player wins. The tournament committee drove Louis and I and our caddies around the par-3 course, through the woods behind the eleventh tee, down the secret little passageways that fit the perfect decorum and traditions of Augusta National, and out to the eighteenth tee.

———

Back again at the eighteenth hole for the second time in less than thirty minutes, I stuck to the plan that I had during regulation play. I would live and die by the driver. Louis and I again both hit perfect drives. At the green, his birdie putt narrowly missed falling into the hole, while my putt never had a chance. So then we headed to the tenth, which was a perfect hole for me because I could slice it right to left in the shape of the dogleg. But my ball didn't cut, and I ended up right into the trees.

My shoulders slumped as I stood aside for Louis to hit his drive. I had ruined another chance at winning a major championship. My thoughts in that moment as I contemplated the difficulty of my next shot were that I might never have another shot at winning a Masters. I was beating myself up. Louis flared his drive and had a shot of more than 200 yards into the green. So as I passed his ball walking down the fairway, I was thinking that if somehow we could make par, we could make it to the next playoff hole. As I was approaching my ball, I noticed that the patrons had created a path in the shape of a hook shot and that I didn't have any tree trouble. I knew I had a shot. When I got to the ball, I knew instantly that this was a shot built for me. I had pulled off shots like this before. This was all in my head. Not even Teddy knew what I was thinking. I understood that many things could have gone wrong, but I was in a much better place than I was a few minutes earlier when my shoulders were slumped on the tee box. I had some time to consider my options. This was match-play now and what Louis did with his approach shot would influence my decision out of the woods. Louis's shot came up short, meaning he would have to pitch back up the hill over a hump in the green. It would be hard for him to stop the ball anywhere near the hole.

———————

I began thinking that I could win with a par. I had 134 yards to the front of the green and 164 to the pin. There was a helpful left-to-right wind. Teddy and I agreed that it was a perfect 52-degree gap wedge. We weren't sure I could hit that club 164 yards, but we knew we weren't going to hit it 180. "This is you, bro," he said as he backed away with the golf bag. He had always told me that I was the painter and that he just held the brushes.

I lose feeling when I can't see where the ball is going. So as I hooked the ball, I lost sight of it because it was coming off so fast. To hook the ball 40 yards, I set up with a closed stance and closed clubface. I rolled my hands and de-lofted the face through impact so that I could hit the ball lower. The shot also required a lot of clubhead speed. The patrons started moving in front of me to see the shot. They were screaming so loud that I couldn't hear anything. People were touching me. One man even slapped me across my back, which felt like an invasion of my personal space, even though he meant no harm. I was fuming about the backslap as we made it back inside the ropes, telling Teddy, "He touched me!" Everything was happening so fast that I still hadn't seen where the ball ended up. I was looking at the front of the green and off to the side. Finally, I asked Teddy, "Where is my ball?"

"It's up by the hole," he said.

Louis still had his chip and we fully expected him to get up and down for par. His chip ran past the hole and his par putt was outside of my birdie try. When he missed his par save, I had two putts to win the championship. I was cautiously optimistic that

I could two-putt from ten feet, but something happened on the Ladies Tour a week earlier that made me take even the shortest putts more seriously. I.K. Kim, one of that tour's top players, had missed a fourteen-inch putt on the seventy-second hole of the ANA Inspiration and then lost in a playoff.

I had watched her meltdown and suddenly I started thinking about that! (If you notice the theme here, my mind is often what gets in my way.) I was so scared. I was trying to baby the putt and get the energy just right in my hands. I lagged it up to the hole to about ten inches. The patrons began to cheer and as I stood over the putt, I felt like I was about to start crying. But I.K. Kim kept popping into my head. Doug Sanders—and the time he missed a three-foot putt to win the British Open—also crept into my head. I motioned with one of my hands for everyone to calm down so that I could concentrate on this last putt. I told myself that I had not won. The world is focused on Bubba from Bagdad, the left-hander who never had a lesson. I didn't even have a routine, but I just continued telling myself to go through my routine. I tried to do everything I would do over that putt if it were the second hole of the first round.

———

The ball traveled those last ten inches true, and tears began to flow almost as soon as it cleared the lip of the hole. In rapid fire, I thought of all the people who told me that I wouldn't make it in golf. I thought about Hiram Cook, who gave me my first club, and Bill Weir, who introduced me to PING. My mother was there to cry with me. We held each other as I told her a simple thank you for what she and my dad had done for me. Ben Crane, Rickie Fowler, and Aaron Baddeley were off the side of the green with their families. It meant so much to me that they came out and watched my playoff. I kept asking, "Why is all of this happening to me?" This moment was like the walk from the woods to the fairway a few minutes earlier—thirty seconds, but it felt like an eternity.

At the press conference following the tournament, I said, "I never dreamed this far." What I meant by that is that like all kids, I had dreamed of hitting a shot to win a Masters. But the dream always ended with the shot. Suddenly I was living moments like that press conference that had never been a part of the dream. I was living moments where I waved and gave high fives to fans. I had never thought about the new car or a house that required a trophy room. What twelve-year-old would even know what any of that means? Nobody knows what fame really looks or feels like until it happens to them. I have always awakened from my dreams, but I was trying to express to those reporters that somehow this one was still going. Sitting in front of media from around the word, I realized that the dream was now complete. This was real life.

As most everyone knows, winning the Masters means you're presented a beautiful green jacket. As the Masters champion you get to take the green jacket home for a year, and after that it has to stay on the grounds of Augusta National Golf Club. I brought that jacket home and stored it in a closet in our house in Orlando. When people would ask about it, I would tell them simply that it was in a closet.

Truthfully, down deep I didn't think that I deserved to be a Masters champion. I wasn't as good as some of these guys. They had gone to top-notch schools and grown up playing on great golf courses. In business they call what I was feeling the "imposter syndrome."

I took the jacket out just a couple of times after completing the media blitz in New York. The first was on the morning after I won the Masters. I landed in Orlando at 3:30 a.m. and I was up a few hours later feeding Caleb, when I wrapped him in the green jacket. I snapped a quick picture, then put the jacket back on its hanger.

It would take a few years for me to grow comfortable wearing the green jacket. I was a Masters champion, but I still had so much work to do—both professionally and personally—before I could hear my name mentioned among the many greats to have won that tournament without feeling queasy.

CHAPTER 13

Expectations—a New Experience

As I slipped my right arm through that green jacket after winning the 2012 Masters, I had no idea just how differently the world would see me, how differently I would come to see myself, or how my life was about to change. Winning the Masters was about so much more than the green jacket or the trophy or gobs of money I earned. You become a different person in the eye of the world and, if you're not careful—which I wasn't—in your own eyes. Becoming famous had its ups and downs, and while I probably could have handled it better—maybe a lot better—at least nobody could say I wasn't warned.

In 2010, Graeme McDowell won the US Open at Pebble Beach. That was the same US Open I had failed to qualify for in the days leading up to my tough-love talk from Teddy. Graeme is not a particularly flamboyant character. He's very down-to-earth and I always thought of him as a guy who sort of had things figured out. After I won, his caddie, Ken Comboy, told Teddy to "get ready for a year and a half of hell." Teddy's reply was something to the effect of, "What are you talking about? We just won the Masters!" The caddie went on to explain to Teddy that the more success you have, the more stress you have. That was the bottom line. You think that winning a major will make things easier, and there will be a lot of exciting opportunities that will open up, but with that victory comes a lot more eyes on you and a world of new things to worry about. When Teddy passed that comment along, I didn't know what he was talking about. It didn't take us long to figure out that Ken had been right.

In fact, the new pressure started minutes after that final hole. After the jacket presentation ceremony at Augusta National, I got in a golf cart and was whisked over to an area where all the media were set up. I had just played four days of the most intense golf of my life, and all I could think about was getting back to Angie and Caleb. But I was just getting started. I did a bunch of interviews for ESPN, the Golf Channel, and other news programs, reliving how I felt about winning and making that amazing hook shot in the playoff. I asked my little entourage, which consisted of my mom, my father-in-law, and my manager, Jens Beck, if they would go back to my rental house and pack up my things, so that the minute I finished up with the media, we could leave.

When I finished my interviews, we jumped on a private plane to Orlando. My manager spent the flight time urging me to skip Orlando and continue on with him to New York City to take advantage of the media opportunities. In a normal year, the Masters champion is invited to appear on all kinds of TV and news shows the Monday after the Masters, and winning it the way I did, with the shot out of the woods and a new baby at home, meant all the usual shows plus many more were asking me to come right away. I told him I was not going until I got to see my wife and baby boy. We bantered about this, and my manager said I needed to strike while the iron was hot. This was going to change my life and provide for my family and so on. I told him that, yes, I understood, but I didn't care. One extra day wouldn't matter. So I got back to my house at 3:30 a.m., took a shower and talked with Angie for a few minutes. Then my head hit the pillow and I suppose I slept a little with my mind still going over shots.

A few hours later at 6:00 a.m., we got up to feed Caleb. And then the phone calls started coming in. I was always careful about who I gave my number to, but there had obviously been a "leak" of some sort because the media was calling me direct instead of going through my agency. One radio station called fifty times. My first official request to my manager after winning the Masters was for him to get me a new cell phone number.

The next day, better rested, Angie told me to "go for it" and I went with my manager to New York to take care of the "business" side of winning the Masters. I went on *The Late Show with David Letterman*. They had wanted me to read a "Top 10 or Not Top 10" list but I told them that wasn't my thing, so they made me a regular guest. I walked around the city with my green jacket on. People recognized me and offered their congratulations. At one point, the phone rang and I stopped in the middle of the sidewalk as the person on the other line said, "This is so and so from the White House. The next voice you hear will be that of President Barack Obama."

I listened for a second and, sure enough, the next voice I heard said, "Hi, Bubba, this is the president."

I said, "Hey, buddy! . . . I mean, hello, Mr. President!"

In setting up publicity events, my team tried to line up some of the less obvious things for a golfer to do, things that would gain exposure to new sponsors. For example, we visited the New York Stock Exchange hoping to draw the attention of major companies and the financial industry who were big players in the golf world. I also wanted to show the world I was more than just the hook shot, more than just a golfer. The year 2012 was also a contract year for me as many of my current sponsorship agreements were set to expire. At the time I was with Travis Matthews Clothing, the watch-maker Richard Mille, Titleist, and PING. After winning the Masters I was also looking for good long-term relationships, and many of the deals I signed were much longer than the industry norms. The impact of the Masters victory really started to hit home as I enjoyed lots of healthy competition among the companies looking to get their logos on my hat, shirt, and bag. The offers to play overseas for appearance money also began to roll in. All of a sudden, I was being asked about playing in China, Japan, Thailand, and all kinds of other places I had never visited. Feeling it was too good to pass up, I started adjusting my schedule so I could make a few of those long trips overseas.

Even before I won the Masters, golf was changing my life by making me more recognizable. I think the reason for this is that golf attracts people from all walks of life. People become passionate about their game and passionate about professional golfers who play the game at the highest level. For example, by 2010, I had already gotten to know Justin Bieber through a common friend, pastor Judah Smith. I also met the actor Mark Wahlberg and quarterback Drew Brees in 2010. I even became friendly with Ellen DeGeneres, who invited me on her show after I pestered her for an invitation on social media.

After the Masters, things jumped into overdrive. I started . . . not exactly running with the fast crowd but definitely being recognized by them. I started getting social media messages from guys like LeBron James, Kevin Durant, and Wayne Gretzky, total icons in their sports and much more successful than I had been. Most of the great athletes in many sports just loved the game of golf.

I'm somebody who has lived his life surrounded by a close circle of friends and family I've known most of my life. I had mixed feelings about my friendships with famous people whose lives I moved into and out of all the time. I've always been used to fairly intense relationships that lasted. The ones I was forming with other "celebrities" tended to be more like a support group of people who respected one another and supported each other's careers and charities in different ways.

For example, while I was in Los Angeles one time, I learned that Durant was staying in Beverly Hills, so I invited him to come hear me deliver some remarks at a new church I had helped fund in LA. At the time, the church was holding service at the Montage Hotel in Beverly Hills. Durant and his team, the NBA's Oklahoma Thunder, were in town to take on the Los Angeles Clippers in the NBA Western Conference Finals. My remarks were going to be a part of the regular Wednesday evening service. I wasn't going to lead a Bible study or anything like that. The pastor would tee me up, and I would talk about some lessons from the Bible that were important to me. The service began at 7:30 that evening and there were about eight hundred people packed into the church. Durant came rolling in and sat in the front row. He bolted right after the service to get back to the team hotel but texted me and thanked me for the message. I texted him back and reminded him that Judah and I were coming to the game. I also asked him whether, after the game was over, I could have his shoes.

Without hesitating, he said, "Yeah, sure, man, no big deal. They're yours." Afterward, I felt as though that must have seemed like the most random request for me to make to him, but I felt that Durant was a bad man, and *I wanted his shoes.* If he had asked me for my golf shoes, I'd have said yes and probably played my best round ever just to feel worthy of giving them to him. And he really hadn't seemed bothered by the request.

At the game the next day, I felt some split loyalties because I was friendly with Doc Rivers, Chris Paul, DeAndre Jordan, and some other Clippers. But as Judah Smith and I sat in the front row to watch the game, there was no question that this would become Durant's game. He scored forty-something points and led the Thunder to win the series. After the game, the crowd was filtering out and Durant was standing in one corner of the court doing interviews. All of a sudden, he began untying his shoes and then walked over in his stockinged feet to Judah and me and handed over his shoes. We all gave each other hugs, then Durant walked off to the locker room. I gave Judah the right sneaker and I kept the left.

We were gazing at our "trophies" when I noticed that Durant had written a Bible verse from Ephesians 3:20: "To him who is able to do immeasurably more than all we ask or imagine, according to his power that is at work within us." In other words, when you've been given a gift by God, you have to work to get every ounce out of it. I keep the shoe next to one I bought from LeBron James for $30,000 to support his "I Promise" school project.

This was the good side of sudden celebrity: feeling financially comfortable enough to buy somebody's old sneakers for thirty grand, flying around the country to go to NBA games and joke around with the world's best athletes. All kinds of organizations were throwing goofy money at me for signing this or that, agreeing to meet with so-and-so, or saying a few words at this event or that event. And I was grabbing all the goofy money with both hands, because that was my duty as a father and husband, right? It wasn't until much later that I would realize that agreeing to do so many of these one-off events, or one-hit wonders, as I like to call them today, would become a real distraction. Unlike my true, long-term sponsors whom I have a real relationship with, the one-hit wonders weren't concerned about my schedule, or my need to practice or rest. Understandably, they were simply taking advantage of the spike in my notoriety, and I was too.

Now I did have a lot of fun too. For example, a couple months after the Masters, I threw out the first pitch at a New York Mets game to kick off the Travelers Championship week. When I called my mom to share the good news, she said, "Your dad would not let you if he were alive," reminding me that he was a Yankees fan and wanted me to play for the Yankees. I knew that was true, but up to that point the AA Pensacola Blue Wahoos were the biggest team to let me throw out a first pitch, so when the Mets asked me, what could I say other than yes? The Mets were playing the Baltimore Orioles the day I threw out the first pitch. When the pre-game ceremonies started, I was hanging out in the visitor dugout talking with the Orioles manager Buck Showalter, who is from my hometown of Pensacola. Well, apparently celebrity guests are not allowed to run out onto the field from the visiting dugout to throw a first pitch. At the last minute, the Mets staff had to sweep me out the back of the visitors' dugout to run through the tunnels under the stands and ensure I emerged, appropriately, from the Mets dugout as I made my way out to throw the first pitch.

The following year, I would get an invite to throw out a first pitch at a Yankees game, and, as you might expect, I said yes. Rain put the kibosh on that game, so I never got to take the mound. But it was still a special day for me. The Los Angeles Dodgers were the visiting team, and their manager was none other than Yankee legend Don Mattingly, my favorite baseball player to watch growing up. Despite the rainout, I was able to visit with Don for twenty minutes at Yankee Stadium. Years later, I would get to visit with Don again at the Baseball Winter Meetings with the staff from the Pensacola Blue Wahoos. If only my dad could have been there that day.

I hadn't grown up dreaming about this kind of life, but it was something a fellow with a rambunctious sense of humor who loved sports could get used to. However, it was starting to butt up against another, more important side of me: the family man and professional golfer.

———

If you know me a little better by now, you know that every upside in my life is likely to carry a downside with it, and recognition certainly produced its downside. While the demands on my time from sponsors, the PGA, and my growing network of influential friends increased, I continued to play a full schedule of tournaments. In 2013, I entered twenty-one tournaments and made eighteen cuts, two more than in the previous year. The problem was that I couldn't manage to finish tournaments among the top few, much less win one. Although I was earning fatter paychecks from sponsors, my earnings from golf were cut in half from 2012, further indication that my game seemed to be taking a hit.

And the truth is, it was. I wasn't getting enough sleep and was tired more often than not. I didn't bring the same energy and focus to practicing or playing. And when I didn't practice as hard, I started missing shots in tournaments that I would have made before. A chip here, a putt there. It added up to a lot of tournaments where I struggled to stay in the top twenty-five and, as often as not, failed to. My troubles were compounded by the fact that every morning at the first tee-off of a tournament, I was introduced as "Your 2012 Masters champion, Bubba Watson!" I was paired with the best players and featured on televised matches. It felt like every shot, every decision, every mistake I made was under a microscope. Since I had won the Masters, a part of me felt I was supposed to win all the time, even if I knew that thought process wasn't rational. As I continued to struggle, people began asking me why—surely something had to be wrong. And then, about halfway through the season when I was still not playing that great, the media quit asking me questions. I guess you could say I was old news.

When this kind of downward spiral took hold, fear began to creep in. As usual, I found it all too easy to run toward the negative thoughts. *Will I ever win another Masters? Will I ever win another tournament? Maybe I'm a one-hit wonder and the Masters was my last hurrah.* There I was: I spent my developmental years playing with a chip on my shoulder, trying to prove to others that I belonged at the top of the game, and now having proved it, I was already feeling pressure to prove that I wasn't a fluke. People had expectations of me now, and I didn't want to disappoint them. Not only was I turning against myself, but the return of my negative attitude was making other people believe I was turning against them as well.

For sure, 2013 was no picnic for Teddy. When Graeme McDowell's caddie warned Teddy about the coming eighteen months, he wasn't necessarily directing his compassion toward me as much as toward Teddy. That caddie had learned firsthand how winning a major changes the way the world treats the professional golfer. How everywhere you go, people want to serve your pro.

"Here, let me carry that for you."

"Your money's no good here." And so on.

Who among us could be treated so like a god living on earth and yet resist starting to believe it, at least a little bit? That's what that caddie had been trying to tell Teddy: The world is going to treat your pro so differently because of what tournament he won, and this treatment will change his behavior. Oh, and you're not going to like it. It's hard to stay humble when the world seems to want to serve you. When everybody says, "Bubba, you're the man!" It's hard not to believe, *Yes, I guess I* am *the man!* And when "the man" starts three-putting or driving balls onto the wrong fairway, he might find it hard to blame himself for his shortcomings.

I think all of that contributed to why I yelled at Teddy during the Travelers Championship after I hit the ball into the water and threw away my chance to win. I received a lot of negative press after that incident. I probably deserved 90 percent of it even though the one I was really mad at was myself, not Teddy, as I have said before. But that was no excuse for the emotional outburst. The problem was that my blood pressure was rising again, and I was working myself into being one stressed-out dude.

My knucklehead days were back. The progress I had made since 2010 had been lost, and if I'm honest, in many ways my attitude was worse than it had been back in 2010. I later learned that Teddy came perilously close to leaving me during 2013, calling his wife on multiple occasions to vent about this or that, saying it was the final straw. Fortunately for me, his wife talked him out of quitting by reminding Teddy that he himself had said I was going through a rough patch, and if he was right, then he needed to stick it out and support his friend.

As the months went by, I found myself being short with complete strangers who happened to want to congratulate me. Practices were normally a relaxed time for me and Teddy, but if somebody came up to me and said, "That was an amazing shot you made at the Masters," I'd shoot back, "Man, that was a year ago. Let me alone so I can win again." I reached a point where I rarely wanted to go out in public. Even trips to the grocery store seemed fraught with risk, as I was certain to be recognized no matter how hard I tried to hide my face behind a box of Cocoa Puffs. It is hard to explain how desperate I was to avoid the never-ending questions about the Masters, the hook shot, and if I was going to win again. By the end of 2013, I was looking for a fresh start.

To help restore balance to my life, I stopped reading the replies to my social media posts and stopped watching the golf news on TV. It was easier to ignore what people said about me if I didn't know what they were saying. After all, if there was anything floating around in the media that I needed to address, my support team would let me know. I also worked on bringing back the fun and hoped it would lead to a good number on Sunday.

"One day, you'll get your life back and start enjoying the game again. When you play with joy and a sense of fun, there's nobody better than you," Teddy told me during this period.

There were others who I reached out to because I admired and trusted them. One was John Solheim, the CEO of my sponsor PING. As the CEO of a big, multigenerational, family-owned company, he knew a thing or two about the pressure of living up to everyone's expectations. He also had high expectations of the people that represented PING.

I told John that without him I could never have turned pro. PING took a chance on me when I first turned professional, and I wouldn't have been able to afford to keep paying to play without them. I told him I was worried about upsetting him with my behavior and poor play. Like a father figure, John was always stern but encouraging and supportive.

I will always fight the traits that make it easy for my mind to go to those dark places. Even with hard work, I know I may never get my mind in the right place 100 percent of the time—but I believe I have made a lot of progress over the years.

CHAPTER 14

My Year of Rejoicing—
Winning a Second Masters

What a difference a year can make. Professional golf takes an enormous amount of physical, mental, and emotional energy to play. It's one of the few sports that consists of nothing but championships every week. Lose your edge or get behind on your sleep, and you can fall behind the eight ball pretty fast! You enter what I call "the fog," a constant state of tiredness and stress where you're going through the motions rather than living and playing with zest. That's what had happened to me in 2013. When the fog came in, there was only one place I wanted to be, and that was out of the public eye. When the cold weather started to set in in the late fall of 2013, I crawled back to our second home at Scottsdale's Estancia Golf Club.

With the course only a couple hundred yards from our home and the mountains framing the course in the distance, it was our perfect refuge to step off the treadmill and regain our lives a little bit. We built our days around golf and eating and playing with Caleb—sometimes all at the same time. We'd walk to the clubhouse for lunch and apologize every time Caleb destroyed the place. We went to birthday parties, and I played with the other members in tournaments held at the club. I was one of the guys again and, gradually, I found that I was able to breathe more easily. I started playing better and finishing some rounds in the sixties, and before I knew it, the fog had lifted.

Following the whirl and negativity of 2013, I decided to dedicate 2014 as "the year of rejoicing," a time to compete hard and always try to improve, but also a time to appreciate my good fortune in life and in golf. From now on, I was going to try harder to emulate my biblical role model, Jesus Christ, and put God first, my wife second, my child third, my friends and family fourth, and golf fifth. I won't say I was completely successful right off the bat, but I did begin 2014 a whole lot better than I ended 2013. In February of 2014, I won the Northern Trust Open at Riviera Country Club with a big weekend comeback, shooting 64 on Saturday and Sunday after barely making the Friday cut. Then I followed that performance with a couple of runner-up finishes, all before the Masters rolled around in April.

And Angie started letting me eat burritos every day again, so I knew that everybody's confidence level was sky-high.

I went into the 2014 Masters in a totally different state of mind than I had in 2012. I had won the Masters before and I had lost it before, and I definitely preferred winning. But I felt more relaxed and focused and less edgy than I had in 2012 and 2013. I wouldn't say that my intensity was any less, but it was a different kind of intensity—more positive. During the practice sessions, I was pretty much lost in the crowds, so I could focus on warming up without media attention or people watching me. Before the tournament started and even once it began, I ignored news reports and TV coverage, a practice I'd started with even before the Masters. My goal was just to keep my head down and stay level: not too energized, not too excited, and not too upset if things happened to not go my way.

On the first day, Bill Haas shot a 68, which gave him a one-shot lead over Louis Oosthuizen, Adam Scott, who was defending champion, and me. It was shaping up to be a hotly contested Masters with eighteen players, including Rory McIlroy, twenty-year-old Jordan Spieth, Fred Couples, and Rickie Fowler within three shots of the lead after the first round. On Friday, I birdied five holes in a row and finished the day with my own 68 and a three-shot lead after thirty-six holes. I was the only player from the top ten after the first round to match or better his score in the second round but fell off a bit on Saturday with 2-over-par 74, tying me for the lead with Spieth going into Sunday's final.

Spieth and I were paired for Sunday, and he quickly moved ahead of me on the second hole with a birdie, and then went up by two after I bogeyed on the third. After some back-and-forth, he was still two up walking off the seventh green. I remember telling myself, *You've been in this situation before and this back nine is gonna be hard. So hit a good tee shot on eight and keep the pressure on.* I knew the back nine on Sunday was where the tournament would be decided, and if I could stay around the lead then I'd have a shot at it.

Spieth ended up losing the lead on the eighth hole where I birdied and he three-putted for a bogey. We were back to a tie. On the next hole, I birdied and Spieth bogeyed again, giving me a two-shot lead. All of a sudden, I had a two-shot lead going into the back nine, and I started talking to myself again. Actually, I was yelling at myself inside my own head. *Okay, don't worry about what anybody's doing. This is hard. This kid doesn't understand the back nine, the energy level of the back nine.* Spieth, who I have enormous respect for, had become "the kid" to me. I was trying to figure out ways to pump myself up. *This is gonna be the most stressful thing he's ever done. And he's young. He's a lot younger than I was when I won for the first time.*

Having given myself the silent pep talk of a lifetime, I bogeyed the tenth hole. Here, Spieth cut my lead down to one with a par. After matching pars on eleven, I was still up one walking to the famous par-3 twelfth hole. As we were walking from the eleventh hole to the twelfth hole, the crowd was getting louder and louder, and all I could think was, *Keep your head down and focus.* On the twelfth, I parred again and Spieth hit the ball in the water. This might have done a lot of guys in, but Spieth made a twenty-foot putt to pull out a bogey. I was feeling a little rattled by his putt, but now I was up two. *Man, I thought I was going to pick up a couple shots. No problem. Okay, all I have to do is birdie the par 5 and I'm hard to beat.*

When we got to the par-5 thirteenth hole, I stepped up to the tee and hit a huge sweeping slice that managed to just miss the trees on the backside of the dogleg. From the tee I could not tell for sure if I had missed the trees, and there was a chance it could have bounced backward into the water or woods, but when I heard the roar of the crowd, I knew it was good, really good. It turned out to be something like 360 yards of near perfection. I could breathe again. Spieth later said he thought it had gone 70 yards out of bounds on the left and just shook his head when we got to where it landed. I used a 56-degree sand wedge to get the ball onto the green and managed a nervous two-putt for a birdie. After Spieth made par, my lead was up to three. Jonas Blixt moved into a tie for second with Spieth.

On the fifteenth, still three strokes ahead of Spieth and Blixt, I drove the ball behind the trees and into some rough. Even though I had a three-shot lead, the last thing I wanted to do was go into some kind of "prevent defense." I was thinking of using an 8-iron up the gap and asked Teddy about it.

"How far to pin do you think it is?" I asked.

"One-eighty over the water and 210 to the pin," Teddy answered.

I wanted to hit it in the bunker beside the green, which is not normally a good place to aim for, but I wanted to get a little closer to the pin. Laying up on the sloping fairway would have left me a very difficult shot with the way I impact the ball with my lob wedge or sand wedge. My mind was racing as I told Teddy, "I think it's a perfect 6-iron if I hit a bullet. It needs to go under the limbs of the tree and then fly over the water. It probably won't stop on the green, but that's not the goal."

"We can make par with a 6-iron, right?" I asked Teddy.

"Right. I guarantee you a par," said the wise one.

I later learned that the TV commentators and perhaps 90 percent of the people watching the tournament thought I was nuts trying to hit that shot. In their eyes, I was putting myself at risk with an unnecessarily aggressive shot. But in our minds, Teddy and I were playing a game of chess. We thought there was a higher probability of making par from the right bunker, or over the green, than there was if I left myself with a 95-yard third shot off a tight lie, on a down-sloping fairway with all sorts of divots, water to go over, and a chance a good wedge shot could still spin back into the water. Teddy and I have talked about that shot and agree that neither of us felt a hint of doubt about whether we could get the ball over the green. We couldn't have cared less about getting a birdie. All we needed was par. If my opponents managed a birdie on the hole, we'd give them the stroke and make it up somewhere else.

My ball landed in the fringe and shot over the green, which

wasn't a surprise. While it left a difficult chip shot, being over the green in two on a par 5 left me with a relatively easy par. Nobody made birdie, so I did my job. We did everything we wanted to do. In my mind, that hole will go down as one of our best-executed moments.

At this point I could breathe a little easier because there were no roars from the crowd, nobody in front of me making birdies. Teddy and I were aiming for the middle of the greens. On sixteen, Teddy was in my ear telling me that if I parred the hole we were probably going to win. If we bogeyed the hole, we still had a great shot at winning. It was his way of telling me to keep the tee shot away from the water, short, and left of the pin, to eliminate the "big number" such as a double bogey or worse. We were trying to stay positive but focused on what our best options for attack looked like. On seventeen, I just missed the bunker and ended up chipping it six feet past the hole. Here, again, Teddy slid up next to me and said, "If you make this shot, we have a three-shot lead going into eighteen. If you miss it, we have a two-shot lead."

They updated the traditional manually operated leader boards fast at every hole so everybody would know where things stood. At the par-4 eighteenth tee, I pulled my 4-wood, which I had designed especially for the eighteenth hole at Augusta. My confidence was soaring. I had to make a five and the other guys had to make a two to stay in it. Our goal wasn't to knock it a mile but to keep it in play, and that's exactly what I did. I hit it right down the middle. I couldn't ask for a better shot. And then I hit a 9-iron onto the green. I've always had a dream of walking up the eighteenth fairway knowing I was going to win and high-fiving everybody before sinking my putt. I told this to Teddy while we were getting ready to walk to the eighteenth green.

"Let's just get the victory first," he advised me. "Let's do this right . . . and then you can go ahead and do anything you want, okay?"

Despite my best efforts to keep myself under control, as I approached the final green, my mind was beginning to spin as I felt the moment of victory approaching. After Spieth missed his first putt, he finished out, letting me take the spotlight. I walked over to Teddy and asked, "I've got four putts now, right?"

"Yes," Teddy said.

And then it was just Teddy and me on the green. I kept asking him, "Is it fast? Is it fast? How fast is it?" I was referring to the condition of the green. I don't even remember making the final putt. I couldn't see straight and had to ask Teddy to read the line to the hole for me. I was acting as though I'd never putted in my whole life. After it went in, I remember bending over to get the ball and standing up to see Angie and Caleb rushing over in my direction. That's kind of when I woke up.

Golf is an individual sport, one in which you focus like a laser on playing within yourself and trying to control your emotions. When it's over, especially if you win, it suddenly just hits you how much you depend on your team—my team are my family and friends—and how much they mean to you. The win means nothing to me without them. My parents were my role models. They worked hard for me and sacrificed, so I wanted to be that role model for my son, on and off the course.

When Angie and Caleb came on the green, I picked Caleb up and started walking around the green and high-fiving everybody I could find, and I kept high-fiving them as we made our way up to where you sign your scorecard. At that moment, I realized that I was living the dream and seeing through the vision very much as I'd imagined it would happen.

———

After grabbing a bite at Augusta National, a bunch of us—Angie, Teddy, Randall, Judah, and his wife, Chelsea—all continued the celebration with a midnight snack at a Waffle House, where I had a grilled cheese and covered hash browns. Unlike the previous Masters, I decided ahead of time to do an end run around the whole New York media circus and book a two-week getaway with Angie. Sometimes the media builds you up so you feel like you're the greatest man alive; other times, it tears you down so you might begin to doubt your own sanity. At that point in my life, I wanted no part of either of these things. But before Angie and I left, I popped in unexpectedly on the *Morning Drive* gang at the Golf Channel, to lay a little Bubba wisdom on the world.

At least, that's what I posted on Twitter. What the visit ended up being was a little different but fun all the same. The crew and hosts were very warm. We talked about what was different for me this time around, and when I got to the part about picking Caleb up in my arms afterward, I started tearing up. I knew one of the show's hosts had recently had her first child and felt like she could understand how proud I felt. She also asked me what I thought of Spieth's play during the tournament, calling attention to some moments on Sunday when he threw his club down and showed his frustration. I told them I had no clue that anything was going on but felt nothing but respect for Spieth at the end of that day.

I didn't think he was immature or anything like that. "Who doesn't get mad?" I said. "He's going to improve on it. It didn't bother me at all. I love the kid to death. . . . It was one of those things where he was trying to win a green jacket, just like me."

After I'd won the Masters in 2012, I sort of "hid" the jacket in my closet. I didn't want to appear in public with it or have lots of people pawing at it. The reason for this was that I had put the tournament on such a high pedestal that I couldn't really enjoy it as much as I might have wanted to. I wanted to show the people who put the tournament together that I understood and respected what the Masters signified to golfers everywhere. And, of course, there was a little part of me that felt unworthy of the jacket—that just maybe it had been a fluke. Two years later, I had gotten over any such squeamishness and decided to use my second green jacket as a platform to help other people.

I wanted to visit all my old schools—my elementary school, middle school, high school, and colleges—and tell the students it doesn't matter where you come from, what your dream is, or what field or endeavor you want to enter, you can make it. It will take a lot of blood, sweat, and tears, but anything is possible. I told them straight up that the green jacket I wore meant that no matter what people say about you, or what people think about you, you can still do it.

The difference between 2012 and 2014 was that I was no longer dumb and innocent, trying to do everything and pretending to be Superman. As for my own obligations to sponsors and others who wanted to pay me boatloads of money, I learned how to say no. I was still getting paid, no mistake about that, but I did it more on my terms. Being a one-time Masters champion is one thing, but when you've won two times within three years, you earn more flexibility to say, "No, I don't think I can do that today!" And those close to me, like Angie, Randall, and Teddy, were also wiser and knew how the game worked.

By the time 2014 drew to a close, I had clocked in my best year ever. I had eleven top-twenty-five finishes and eight top-ten finishes. I finished in the top five on four occasions and won my second Masters. I also finished second in earnings, my highest-ever finish on the money list. My world golf ranking went from twenty-sixth in 2013 to fourth in 2014. Best of all, I had proven to myself that 2012 was not a fluke. Bubba Watson from Bagdad had established himself at the top of his game not once, but twice. I think my dad would have been proud. He'd have to be working extra hard in heaven if he was ever going to catch me now. But returning to the top didn't come without a price.

CHAPTER 15

Will I Ever Be Good Enough?

I was sitting across the desk from Ben Crane wondering, *What did I do this time?* I had just finished playing a practice round for the 2014 BMW Championship at the Cherry Hills Country Club in Colorado and he had mentioned several times in the days before that he wanted to talk to me.

I asked Teddy what it was all about. "Why does he want to talk to me? Why does he need a separate room to talk? Why can't we talk in public?" Teddy just shrugged, but I later discovered that he must have had a pretty good idea of what Ben was up to.

Now, here we were. He began by telling me that he was coming from a place of love and that, more than anything, he wanted me to be careful. That my friends didn't like being around me. That I had turned cold or ugly at the drop of a hat. He was concerned that in my pride and stubbornness—he didn't use those exact words, those are my words—to fix things myself, I was losing sight that God was the one who did the changing when we let ourselves get close to him.

He tried to point me toward the gospel by saying that we're all broken and desperately in need of grace from God and each other. He said that I was loved and didn't have to prove myself to anybody to be loved. If I could see that, I would experience a sense of freedom. If I felt the love in my heart, I would act lovingly toward others. It wouldn't be a matter of trying to behave in a way that looked good to people, which was just hypocrisy.

This wasn't like 2010, when Teddy rolled the dice and confronted me about my attitude on the golf course and how I was living and dying with golf more than anything else. Ben wasn't concerned about my attitude on the course, or how it impacted my play. I wasn't living and dying with every shot; I was playing some of the best golf of my life. Instead, Ben was concerned about how I was treating others, including people I thought of as my friends. In short, he was saying I needed to be a better person, to open up my heart and truly connect with those around me. One issue he raised in particular was how I picked on other players.

When you play golf as much as I do with a lot of guys, you start to feel comfortable ribbing each other. It's a natural part of the game . . . that is, until you cross the line. Maybe somebody teases you when you make a bad shot or brags about "how it's done." If you know each other well enough, you know each other's weaknesses and can offer a good comeback. It might sting a little, but it isn't mean-spirited or ugly. You just have to know where to draw the line.

Well, apparently, I *didn't* know where to draw the line.

So my friends and other golfers started taking their complaints about me to Teddy, who knew far better than they did just how frosty and mean I could be. But Teddy had all he could handle with our relationship, much less everybody else's, so he would remind them of what the Bible said: If you have a problem with your brother, go to your brother. If he doesn't listen, get two people and go to your brother. If he still doesn't listen, get the

I have always loved being outside.

I always wanted superpowers.
Doesn't every kid dream
of being Superman?

Golf tournaments were the
best part of summer.

The knickers only came out
on tournament days.

Molly Watson

Payne Stewart was my favorite
player growing up. I wore this
hat so I could be like him.

Playing a junior tournament with
Randall. I think I was thirteen or
fourteen in this picture since I
had stopped wearing knickers.

Molly Watson

I have always wanted to
represent the USA!

American Junior Golf Association

Courtesy of
the AJGA

Growing up, nothing was too
bright or colorful for me to wear.

A good boy and a not-so-good boy. Not saying which is which.

Notice the colorful custom putter shaft painted by my dad. Back then no one would make me a pink driver shaft.

Courtesy of the AJGA

Yeah, I guess I've always liked the color pink.

Courtesy of the AJGA

Even as a junior I loved team events.

Our wedding day. So glad Mom and Dad got to share it with Angie and me.

One of the last times I saw Billy Weir, the retired PING salesman who introduced me to PING and the Solheim family. He was a great man.

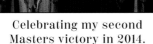

Celebrating my second Masters victory in 2014.

First pitch at a Pensacola Blue Wahoos game after winning the 2014 Masters. I asked Quint Studer to let me buy part of the team that day.

Early days with Caleb.

Angie with young Caleb.

Chilling with baby
Dakota and her proud
brother, Caleb.

Dakota's third
birthday. I
think she had
already snuck a
handful of icing.

Getting ready for the Masters Tournament Par 3 Contest. One of our family's favorite traditions.

Uga is a lot heavier than you think!

Caleb's VPK graduation. Kids grow up too fast!

With my mom in the Wahoos locker room.

Not everyone gets to dress up
like a real-life teddy bear.

We love the Jockey
Being Family
Foundation and helping
families through the
adoption process.

The whole family loves supporting the
Studer Family Children's Hospital.

Dakota may love Bubba's Sweet Spot more than I do.

Nothing beats being a dad and helping out the team.

Caleb loves dressing up like an elf and helping with my annual Bubba Claus videos every December.

It's hard to beat a family day at Pensacola Beach.

I may be a golfer, but Angie and I both love basketball. We love to go to games when we can.

whole church and go to your brother (Matthew 18:15–17). Teddy told them to put their big-boy pants on and tell me to my face.

Ben was the first one to actually do it.

It was tough to hear that from someone I respected so much as both a Christian and a friend. In fact, it was tough enough that I chose not to listen very carefully to what Ben was actually saying. My memory of our conversation mostly involves me sitting there and staring across the table at Ben and letting his amazing gift to me go in one ear and out the other. This is not easy to admit, even now. In reality I should have seen that conversation as a flashing red light, telling me to stop and assess my behavior. But I didn't. Before long it would become clear that more people felt the way Ben did than I realized.

At the 2015 Masters I was the defending champion, which many people would naturally assume to be a peachy spot to occupy, but my own experience in 2013 suggested otherwise. Still, I must have learned a thing or two from that earlier experience because I was playing a lot better going into the 2015 Masters than I was in 2013. I was also working nonstop and trying to make my wife happy and take care of my family that I've been blessed to have. That was the whole goal.

In the weeks leading up to the Masters, ESPN did an anonymous poll of around one hundred professional golfers on a variety of topics. One of the questions had to do with which of their professional colleagues they'd be least likely to help out in a parking lot brawl. My name headed this unfortunate list. I remember responding with a smart-aleck retort: "Well, at least they believe I can defend myself." But I'll admit it, it was a gut punch. While I would like to say it was the poll that eventually led to my being regularly tagged as a "divisive" player on the tour, it wasn't the poll's fault. After all, the ESPN poll was a reflection of some of the things Ben Crane had been trying to warn me about months before. There was some truth to it.

The media weren't the only ones who hadn't forgotten about my outbursts at the 2013 Travelers Championship involving Teddy or all the times I was short with people simply trying to make friendly small talk. I remembered and regretted each and every incident. Even after the poll came out, it took some time for me to truly accept what others were saying.

Maybe there is a reason guys said what they did in the poll, I thought. Maybe Ben was speaking for more people than I realized. I still wasn't completely sure what he had said, but it was clear he was right.

As the weeks went by, I began to feel that it didn't matter whether I was a Christian or not. We all needed to have accountability partners who kept us in line and felt safe enough to speak up and tell us when we were messing up. It wasn't just a case of Teddy and Angie and a handful of tour players and caddies who "didn't understand me." It was time for me to take responsibility for my own behavior. I needed to get away from believing that I held all the answers to my problems and that no one could help me.

I'd spent the better part of my life doing what a lot of folks do: telling myself a story about who I was and how I was supposed to act. I was Bubba from Bagdad who never had a golf lesson and didn't fit in with the "established" golfing community, but who worked his way into the upper echelon of his sport by devoting himself to his craft. Bubba the individualist who didn't ask favors of other people but was always generous when it came to supporting his own and other people's charities. Bubba Watson who relied on nothing but his own two hands to turn the $500 his parents gave him to enter his first mini tournament into millions as a PGA professional and to become a two-time Masters champion. Bubba, the guy who tried so hard to please everybody that he could make himself crazy and wind up pissing everybody off.

The problem with these kinds of narratives is that they can make you deaf to what's really going on in the world around you. It makes you think that your way is better than everybody else's because you're special. And when you've become famous, the world around you will reinforce this feeling. At least for a while. At least while you're still on top. I don't know about other callings, but this brand of arrogance gets professional athletes in trouble, ruining their lives in ways they couldn't imagine.

Ben's conversation planted a seed in me, but I didn't really water that seed and let it grow until after the ESPN poll. Ultimately, I was inspired to redouble my efforts to be a better person, and I made a pact with my close friends that we should give each other the freedom to love on one another enough to say something when we see it.

There is a rather large group of guys on the PGA Tour that put together a Bible study group, and many of my friends participate. The group serves as a ready-made band of brothers who are there to hold each other accountable. It's gotten to the point where the group doesn't wait for problems to show up. Teddy likes to use the analogy of a leaky roof. "If it's raining, call a roofer. Don't wait until there's mold and mildew, and we have to call a roofer, a carpenter, a sheet rocker, and an electrician to fix the damage that happens when you ignore the rain," he says.

But you need to give each other permission to be honest, which is another way of saying you have to agree to love on one another.

I also decided to make some other changes in my life. During my stretch of good play in 2014 and 2015, I had started once again to let golf and the obligations that go with it take over my life. Real or not, I was applying a lot of pressure on myself to excel on the course, for the media and for my partners. For probably the first time in my career, I had started watching the world rankings on a weekly basis. While I was managing better than I did in 2013, I needed to learn how to say no more often. Not to people seeking an autograph or a word of acknowledgment after offering me some well-intentioned encouragement, but to allowing golf to consume all my focus and energy. To the growing lists of things that sponsors wanted me to do that earned me more money but distracted me from actually playing the game and spending time with the people I loved. To feeling guilty for skipping a tournament and taking a week off to go on a little vacation with Angie while Caleb's grandparents looked after him.

In 2012, just weeks after my first Masters victory, I had said no, skipping the Players Championship, an event so big it is often called the fifth major. I did it because I needed to be there for my son so that he could have a father's touch and voice all around him. The media questioned that decision as did some of my friends, but I knew it was the right thing to do at the time. Somehow, during 2016, I had lost my sense of balance in life and had become somebody other than the man I wanted to be.

Now don't get me wrong, I loved being on top of the game, showing up to a tournament, and truly feeling like I could win if I even played halfway decent. But the world was moving fast, and it was easy to lose track of the days, weeks, and months that seemed to fly by. It was hard to believe it had been five years since my first win at the 2010 Travelers Championship, yet it was also hard to believe it had *only* been five years. Two Masters, two adoptions, countless run-ins with the media, and a new life that seemed to bear little resemblance to anything I had experienced before eventually began to wear on my soul.

When I was a child, I didn't want to upset my parents or friends. And when I became an adult, I didn't want to upset my sponsors or my manager or Angie or my close friends. I didn't want to upset the fans. I had tried so hard not to upset everyone that I ended up ticking off every last one of them. It was hard not to wonder: Would I ever be good enough?

CHAPTER 16

Our Second Adoption

After we adopted Caleb in 2012, we felt so blessed to have a new member in our family. After I won the Masters, things started changing so fast that we didn't think too much about adopting another child. We had not planned to adopt again right away because we wanted Caleb to grow up a little bit. But things moved faster than we had imagined.

The year 2014 was a whole new ballgame. I was back to playing good golf and felt like life was just plain good, so we started the process of adopting a sibling for Caleb. All we knew was that we wanted a girl and wanted her to be as young as possible. After filing with some adoption agencies in the spring of 2014, the waiting process started all over again.

With a win at the 2014 Masters behind us and me scheduled to play tournaments in China and Japan in the fall, Angie and I had a heart-to-heart about whether I should go or not. We decided we should take a lesson from our first go-round with Caleb and not wait around. We'd learned firsthand about the heartache that comes when you're told that the birth mother has chosen another family instead of you, and how a baby can literally be taken away from you up to the last minute. Being an athlete, Angie said, "Look, we've got to keep living our lives and pray for the best. We've already planned your year, and this is your profession. You need to play. Why wouldn't you want to go to the HSBC World Golf Championships in China and on to Japan to play on a course you love, right by Mount Fuji?" Besides, we had friends and family we could count on to help us out if things got too crazy.

I had to admit, Angie drove a hard bargain, so I committed to making the seventeen-day trip to China and Japan.

As fate would have it, right as I left for China, we got a call saying there was a baby girl soon to be born in California, and the birth mother had selected us. We knew the struggles of adoption and didn't want to get too confident, and thought, *Hey, even if this one doesn't go through for us, there are thousands upon thousands of other children looking for homes, right?* Halfway around the world, I kept in constant contact with Angie, as she prepared the house for a new member of our family. While part of me wanted to withdraw from the tournament and jump on the first flight home, we had discussed such a scenario in advance, so I stayed to play golf and fulfill my obligations.

I felt great at the HSBC in China. I was firing on all cylinders and had my physical therapist with me and Randall and Teddy. Like usual we were goofing around and playing some tennis and going to the gym during off times. I was in constant touch with Angie, and even when I was playing golf, my thoughts were on getting to go home to a new family and experiencing all the new baby stuff all over again. I felt torn between being so far away from her and Caleb at this time in our family's life and my commitment to "play my play," but somehow, my mental state was so relaxed that I couldn't miss a shot for the whole week.

On the last day, I had a one-shot lead going into the par-3 seventeenth hole. After hitting my tee shot into the greenside bunker, I managed to make a mess of things and ended up making a double bogey. I would have become distraught in other frames of mind, but I just shrugged it off. On the par-5 eighteenth hole, I knocked my second shot into the greenside bunker. At that stage I needed a small miracle to keep my hopes of winning the tournament alive, and what do you know, I holed out from the greenside bunker for an eagle three. To this day, the roar of the crowd when the ball went in the hole remains one of the loudest moments I have ever experienced on the golf course. I can't think of any other shot I have played, including the hook shot at Augusta, that has resulted in such an overwhelming rush of adrenaline and joy. That hole out earned me a spot in a playoff that I would eventually win. Looking back, it is hard not to feel as if there was some sort of divine intervention that day.

Two days later, our baby girl was born. After a child is born, the hospital gives the adopted baby time to bond with the new family in the Adopt Out Room while the birth mother recovers in another hospital wing. Caleb came in and looked at her through the nursery glass. We have a picture of him wearing a sticker that says "Big Brother" and just looking through the glass at her.

Caleb already had his name before we adopted him, but this time around we got to name our child. I had this crazy idea in my head that we should follow the alphabet. We had A, B, and C, so I wanted a name beginning with D. I proposed "Dakota." Angie wasn't so sure. The movie *Fifty Shades of Grey* had just been released, and the last person Angie wanted people to think about when they heard the name Dakota was the movie's star character, Dakota Johnson. But I reminded Angie that Dekoda Watson was also the name of an ex–Florida State University linebacker and professional football player!

So the name Dakota Hope Watson stuck.

The process of adopting Dakota went a lot faster than it had with Caleb, who took almost six months to finally adopt once we established a Florida residence. But Dakota had her own little set of hiccups. We had to go through a lawyer to get final custody, which meant we had about a month of keeping Dakota under wraps while the paperwork came through. During that month, the Tavistock Cup was played at Isleworth, where we lived. That meant that keeping Dakota under wraps required a bit more effort than expected. Any other year, we might have invited other players and their wives to the house. But not so that year, with one exception. As previously planned, Rickie Fowler stayed in the guest apartment over our garage during the tournament, so he met Dakota long before the rest of the world. I still have a picture of Rickie holding Dakota that week. He had also stayed with us right after we adopted Caleb, and it seemed only natural to have him there in the early days with Dakota. To this day, I feel Rickie and my family have a special bond. He has always been great with our children and always seems to know how to make them smile.

The world would finally learn of Dakota when I posted a picture on social media a few days before Christmas.

———

Our children have been such blessings in our lives that I have felt I ought to use whatever success I've enjoyed in golf to serve as a platform for removing the stigmas around adoption. In 2015, Angie and I served as spokespersons for the National Council for

Adoption, a non-profit organization with a mission to meet the diverse needs of all those touched by adoption. In that year alone, an estimated 18,000 infants and more than 76,000 older children were adopted. However, more than 101,000 children were still waiting to be adopted, according to the US Department of Health and Human Services. As spokespersons, our role was to raise awareness about the positive option of adopting and advocating for children waiting to be adopted. We filmed some public service announcements and served as cochairs of the NCFA's 35th Anniversary Great Expectations Gala, where Angie served as the keynote speaker, leaving barely a dry eye in the house.

In 2018 I signed with the Jockey Being Family Foundation as an ambassador to raise awareness for the foundation and its goal of supporting adoptive families. Jockey Being Family is Jockey International's corporate charitable initiative, which provides resources and support to post-adoption organizations to strengthen adoptive families once an adoption is finalized. Post-adoption services frequently requested by adoptive families include information, respite care, parent support groups, and referrals to medical professionals.

In addition to supporting these organizations financially, I have also discussed adoption in countless interviews and gatherings. My goal is to share my experiences and thoughts about adoption and maybe that way dispel some of the misconceptions about it. For many years nobody talked about adoption. I hate to say it this way, but I believe many men felt ashamed of adopting because not conceiving their own child would reflect poorly on their "manliness." I've never felt like less of a man for adopting. I look at Caleb and Dakota, and I don't think of anything else except that God made these children in somebody else's womb for us. There are so many beautiful kids out there who didn't ask to be put in a certain situation; they're just looking for love. It's a blessing for Angie and me that these beautiful kids are now ours and we get to raise them. Winning golf tournaments is great, and I hope to keep doing it, but I know that the most important thing I'm going to do in this lifetime is be a dad to Caleb and Dakota.

I feel blessed to have kids, but the older they get, the more responsible I feel about setting a good example for them. My little boy and girl are always watching me, so I need to be mindful of what I want them to learn from me. This, in turn, means I have to constantly work on being a better person, a better husband, a better dad, and a better colleague.

Someday, the kids of today will be in charge of the planet and do great things. But they need the love and support of a family. I feel very lucky to be the son of Molly and Gerry Watson, who sacrificed so much to give me the opportunities to pursue my dreams. Now I want to pay their gift forward to the next generation. Kids waiting to be adopted don't ask to be where they are or to be put in your family. It's up to us. Who knows, maybe there's a kid out there who will one day cure cancer but may not get a chance to unless he's taken care of.

We don't view Caleb and Dakota as our adopted kids. We view them as our kids. But as we've done more public events supporting adoption and taken Caleb with us (Dakota is still too young), he's begun to notice that some kids don't look anything like their parents. We've talked to Caleb about how we adopted him and how children like him are protected in their mothers' tummies and then given to adoptive parents who care for them.

I don't try to be our kids' best friend. I try to be a role model for them, teach them right from wrong, and get them on a positive path. We haven't tried to hide the kids from their birth families either. When they are older, it will be up to them to decide what type of relationship they want to have with their birth mom and dad. Both Caleb and Dakota's birth mothers know who the Watsons are these days, and Angie keeps in contact with them with occasional emails and photos. It was hard for her at first, but she grew to appreciate the sacrifice birth mothers make and what's behind some of these difficult decisions they have to make.

In the first couple years, we did not have much contact with Caleb's birth mom, but after Dakota came along, we began to realize that some level of communication with the birth parents was good for all involved. Angie told me that sending communications has made our relationship with the birth families a lot more open, and I think it's helped everybody feel they made the right decision for these babies. At the same time, the relationship does not include contact between the children and the birth mothers. That isn't likely to be in the cards until Caleb and Dakota are old enough to make that decision by themselves. Right now, our priority is to make sure that Caleb, and eventually Dakota, know that their birth mothers loved them enough that they wanted to help find the best situation for them. I want them to know that we chose them because they're so special.

Like all children, they will eventually grow up and be free to leave home and make their own way in the world. We hope that we have given them the same gifts of love and support we got from our parents and that this will serve them well in their decisions.

CHAPTER 17

Coming Home

When Angie and I left Pensacola in 2008 to live in Scottsdale, we did so for several reasons. Arizona was more central to the PGA golfing scene and would reduce travel time to the West Coast, where lots of events are played. We loved the community and upscale golf courses, and even found a local church we loved to attend when we visited the area. But most of all, we wanted to start our life together, and to do that we needed to create a little space between our marriage and "Bubba Land" in Pensacola. We needed to go someplace where neither of us was the "insider" who knew everybody, and Scottsdale fit the bill.

I never thought about the move as temporary or permanent. It was just something that seemed natural for us to do. In 2012, the process of adopting Caleb answered this question for us by requiring us to move back to Florida, which was Caleb's state of adoption. So we headed to Orlando, looked at something like fifty houses, and ultimately bought Tiger Woods's beautiful lakefront home in Isleworth. That got us part of the way back home, at least to my home. But it took developing relationships with a couple of remarkable people for our living situation to come full circle.

It was in 2014 that I first met a gentleman by the name of Quint Studer who had become a true legend and local hero around Pensacola because he was investing millions upon millions of dollars in the city, driving a major revitalization of downtown Pensacola. Quint often took on projects others would not touch, such as rehabbing old, dilapidated buildings, because while others may have been in it just for the money, Quint only had one goal: to improve the quality of life in Pensacola.

Unless you get to know Quint, it is hard to explain how unique of a person he is. He has been a special education teacher and a CEO at a major hospital, and he's the founder of a very successful health-care consulting company, Studer Group. While he isn't a Pensacola native, I suspect he has done more good for his adopted home than anyone else over the last forty-plus years. He is also the majority owner of the Blue Wahoos baseball team, an AA minor league team then affiliated with the Cincinnati Reds of MLB.

The Blue Wahoos's first year in Pensacola was 2012, and after I won the Masters, I went and threw out a first pitch. Naturally, when I won the 2014 Masters, I went back to throw out another first pitch, this time while wearing the green jacket I had been too nervous to wear on the mound the first time. I did not meet Quint the first time around, but the second time around we spent some time talking and getting to know each other under the stadium. During that conversation Quint said something like, "Let me know if I can ever do anything for you." I quickly replied, "I would love to own part of the team."

I am not sure if Quint realized I was truly serious about buying part of the team, but the next day I asked Randall if he would follow up with Quint. Randall was quick to tell me that he would follow up, but not to get my hopes up because Quint didn't need any equity partners (that might have been the first time I ever heard the word *equity* in regard to owning a company). It took some time for the two of them to connect, but after a few months they did finally meet in person, at the Pinehurst US Open of all places.

To my amazement, it turned out that Quint was willing to let me buy part of the team. The way he saw it, the Blue Wahoos were a symbol of the progress being made revitalizing Pensacola. After all, the new stadium built for the team had helped accelerate the economic development downtown. He also felt I could help the Blue Wahoos become more of a national brand, much like the Durham Bulls in North Carolina had become. Quint describes himself as "a teacher desperate for students," and so when we got together, he asked me why I wanted to own a piece of the team. He liked my answers, and his teaching began!

I told him that I wasn't out to make tons of money—a good thing since minor league baseball generally doesn't. This partnership, I told him, was about more than money. Baseball was part of my childhood and meant a lot to me and to my family. I told him how my mom used to play catch with me in the yard and how passionate my dad was about the game, to the point he always wanted me to become a baseball player. I told him that my main goal in being an owner was to give back to the community that made me who I am. I wanted to give my name, hard work, and money to help build up and sustain the place where I had pursued all my dreams growing up. As a family man I wanted to help create a safe, family-oriented place for people to go and be entertained and forget their worries for a while. He especially liked hearing that I didn't consider myself to be a business expert just because I was a golf expert. Finally, I shared that I wanted mentors who could teach me how to run a business and also how to support a community.

Over the years, our philanthropic interests have aligned a few times, but none were bigger than the expansion of the Children's Hospital at Sacred Heart. Having been born at Sacred Heart, expansion of the Children's Hospital was something I supported from day one. Not surprisingly, Quint and his wife, Rishy, were the project's biggest supporters, often helping to recruit other donors for the project. To get an idea of just how much support Quint and Rishy provided the hospital, all you have to do is consider that today the new, expanded hospital is known as the Studer Family Children's Hospital. On May 4, 2019, Caleb and I woke up early and went up to the hospital to help transfer patients from the old facility to the new facility for its first day in operation. I will never forget the excitement I saw in the patients and hospital staff that day. By the time the hospital was finished, we felt we had helped create a legacy that would survive the ups and downs of everyday life and help people for years and years to come. We felt like we were part of something bigger than ourselves. Of all the philanthropic projects I have supported, the Studer Family Children's Hospital has been the most fulfilling. I am still involved with it today, and if you happen to google it, you may notice that the address is 1 Bubba Watson Drive.

One of the biggest lessons life has taught me is how quickly things can turn for the better or worse. As I began to get involved with the Blue Wahoos, Angie and I started visiting Pensacola frequently, and we often stayed at a little townhouse Quint owned downtown. Over time, both Angie and I fell in love with the coffee shops, restaurants, and parks sprinkled throughout downtown. One day, we'd stopped to grab a coffee and breakfast when Angie surprised me by saying, "You know what? I think I could live in this city, Bubba." I *might* have put our house on the market that afternoon. Going home made sense to me. Now it seemed to make a lot of sense to Angie as well. It took us a few months, but we eventually found a house off of Scenic Highway and by early 2016 we were back living in Pensacola.

As my mentor, Quint kept me humble by telling me he couldn't count how many doctors he knew who started businesses and failed. "It's not enough to be smart or have a great product or service," Quint used to tell me. "*Customer service* is part of the product." One of the ways we implement this credo is to honor a group of Blue Wahoo employees at each game who have excelled at making the experience of supporting the Wahoos better for our customers. During the fifth inning, the honorees line up on the dugout and someone from the executive team hops up there with them and gives them a little pin. It may sound like a minor thing, but the staff love it, and we're connecting the dots by recognizing employees in front of their customers. Our mission is to improve the quality of life in Pensacola. That may sound bold for a baseball team, but I think we've done it.

Most people are unaware of how minor league baseball operates. The major league team—starting in 2021, we are now with the Florida Marlins—manages and pays the salaries of the players, coaches, doctors, trainers, and other athletic staff. From the Marlins's perspective, our job as their AA affiliate is to ensure their AA players have a great facility to play where they can train and continue to gain the experience needed to prepare themselves to make it in the big league. It is kind of like the Nationwide Tour I used to compete in.

While the Marlins are responsible for the players' development and on-field performance, we handle just about everything else. For example, we maintain the field, market the team, and sell tickets, food, and sponsorships. We also plan, host, and arrange hundreds of non-baseball events at the stadium every year. We typically have around twenty-five year-round employees but can balloon up to more than two hundred on game days. That's a significant ramp-up and can provide quite a logistical challenge.

During the COVID-19 pandemic, the entire 2020 baseball season was canceled. The vast majority of minor league teams significantly reduced their staff simply to survive the lost season. However, with the Blue Wahoos, we took another route. Part of our thinking was to keep revenues coming in, but we also wanted to find ways of keeping our full-time staff employed during the pandemic. Unlike many businesses, the Blue Wahoos did not lay off any of our full-time employees despite not having a baseball season. That may have surprised some people, but when you consider that the Wahoos's mission is to improve the quality of life in Pensacola, it's easy to understand why we wanted to stand by our staff. Of course, keeping everyone meant we had to get creative in order for the stadium to remain in use, and get creative we did. For example, Quint's daughter Mallory came up with the idea of renting out the stadium as an Airbnb. For $1,500 a night, renters could access the clubhouse, a special-purpose bedroom set up with ten beds for guests (four bunk beds and two queen beds), as well as two flat-screen televisions and a kitchenette with a fridge, freezer, coffee maker, and microwave. Guests also had access to the batting cages (bats, balls, and helmets were provided), the field, and the rest of the stadium. As the first sports stadium available for rent on Airbnb, the idea drew national and even international attention. Of course, my family spent a night at the stadium—somebody had to test it out, right? We also offered movie nights, trivia nights, outdoor happy hours, and more. We even set up a nine-hole disc golf course on the field and invited the public to come play.

We also doubled down on outreach to the community during those difficult times. All told, the team contributed over one thousand hours of community service in 2020. After hurricane Sally hit Pensacola in the fall of 2020, our staff also spent over six hundred hours helping clear debris.

Baseball America's Bob Freitas Award is generally considered the most prestigious award an affiliated baseball team can win. It is the gold standard for whether a team is helping the community and creating a healthy workplace. I am proud to say that the Blue Wahoos have been recognized as the AA "Organization of the Year" and winner of the Bob Freitas Award twice. The first time was in 2016, and I had the good fortune of accepting the award on behalf of our entire organization at the famous Winter Meetings. The second time we won was 2020. I still can't believe how lucky I am that Quint and Rishy allowed me to be a part of the organization. A few years after I became an owner, we welcomed NFL Hall of Famer and Pensacola native Derrick Brooks into the ownership group.

In the summer of 2016, I partnered with the Studers on a second business, and we opened Bubba's Sweet Spot. It's a small candy and ice cream store located on Palafox Street in downtown Pensacola, just a few blocks from the Blue Wahoos Stadium. The shop came to be after we realized that both Rishy and I had visions of creating something fun and family-friendly that would make kids' eyes grow big when they walked in.

I also see the shop as a little piece of downtown Pensacola's revitalization. The shop is popular with families and visitors strolling around the historic downtown and seeing the sights. But the shop isn't just for kids. We make all kinds of fudge and chocolate-covered treats that I often refer to as the "adult candy." In the evenings, we are a popular dessert spot for couples who eat dinner at one of the many downtown restaurants. The shop also provides a few good jobs in a town that can always use a few more good jobs. When we first opened my mom worked at the shop. While many guests had no idea my mom was the one helping them, some would figure it out after seeing the pictures on the back wall that showed us hugging on the tenth green at the conclusion of the 2012 Masters Playoff. After a few years, she left the candy shop and started working at a small driving range I own, where the pace of things is a bit slower.

Sandy Sansing became another one of my business mentors that same year. Sandy owns a growing collection of car dealerships in greater Pensacola. Back in the eighties, he used to ride elephants in his commercials. He is also a generous supporter of youth sports, especially golf, and sponsors junior golf tournaments that I competed in as a kid. Having gotten a taste of the business world through my ventures with Quint, I suggested to Randall that it might be fun to get in the car business. As I had done with Quint, I asked Randall to reach out to Sandy and see if there might be a way to partner with him one day. I should note that Angie wasn't really excited about the prospect of me getting in the car business at first. Over the years, I had developed a bit of a habit of buying cars, and I didn't always keep them all that long. I really didn't drive that much either since I was on the road half the time. So it was a bit of a running joke that I never changed the oil in my car, I just got a new one.

I knew Angie didn't think I needed to buy so many cars,

so it wasn't a shock when she balked at the idea of me buying three hundred cars all at once. Fortunately, when we moved back to Pensacola, we had met Sandy's two children, Stephanie and David, through our church. They are close to our age and our families have spent a lot of time together. Her familiarity with the entire Sansing family and the knowledge that David was actively involved in the dealership's day-to-day played a big part in helping ease her concern. I guess you could say she trusted them to not let me do anything too crazy.

In addition to our connections through the church, our families also had golf in common. As a lifelong golfer who played in college, Sandy can more than hold his own on the course. He is one of my most frequent playing companions. He and David have also helped me develop a love for fishing, something I would never have imagined I would take to in the past. As much as I have grown to love fishing, I still won't let them take the boat too far out to sea. The rule is that I have to be able to see land!

As my friendship with Sandy and his family was growing, he learned that there was a car dealership in Milton, just a few miles from my childhood home in neighboring Bagdad. The owner wasn't from Pensacola and was looking to sell. Armed with the knowledge that I was keen to get into the car business, Sandy asked if I would be interested in buying the dealership with him, so we bought it and called our new dealership Sandy and Bubba's Milton Chevrolet. The day we bought the store I had no idea how the car business worked. It took a while for me to develop an understanding of how all the departments, such as new cars, used cars, parts, and service, impacted one another. Going in, I placed all my faith in Randall and Sandy in terms of deciding if it would be a good deal, but I have truly enjoyed learning how it works.

Like Quint, Sandy is very good at what he does. One of Sandy's favorite sayings is that business is all about people, people, and people, and when you think about it, he is right. It really doesn't matter if we are talking about a car dealership, a candy shop, or a baseball team; in the end a business is only as good as its people.

While Sandy and Quint don't always say things the same way, I have found that they have a lot in common. For example, they are both adamant that you have to hire the right people and provide them with good training and support. They also recognize that supporting the community is important.

Like Quint and Rishy, the Sansing family is active philanthropically. For example, they were also big supporters of the Studer Family Children's Hospital. David Sansing even sits on the board of the hospital.

In 2018, I bought a local driving range that had been around since 1991 and was getting run down. The owner wanted to get out, so rather than let the business just disappear, I bought it. I didn't know exactly what I would do with it, but if nothing else, it would be a place I could go to hit some balls by myself like I used to do as a kid. In many respects it is little more than a neighborhood driving range, but it is also a place where countless children and adults have learned the game of golf, and that is something I appreciate and want to maintain. Unlike the candy shop, I didn't want to put my name on the range. Instead we named it Pensacola Golf Center in recognition of its role as part of the local golf community. My longtime friend Gabe Sauer runs the range day-to-day with help from Randall. We do not enforce a strict dress code: if you want to practice in cut-off jeans and a tank top, have at it. I have never been one for formalities. We have estimated that as much as 10 percent of the customers show up without their own clubs, so we simply let them borrow some old clubs to hit their bucket of balls.

When we first purchased the range, we wanted to knock down the building and replace it with something much bigger and fancier. As fate would have it, we ran into a lot of permitting problems and had to eventually scrap the plans for a new building. With any luck, by the time you are reading this, we will have completed the major renovation that is currently underway.

I have always tried to ensure that Bubba Watson wasn't just a name on a sign or in a flyer, but you have to keep in mind that playing golf is still my day job. While I like to keep close tabs on the companies, my business partners are the ones who really run things day-to-day, and Randall serves as my eyes and ears when I am away. Before I started investing in companies, I made a deal with Randall to always do it together, and he has stakes in all my companies. Having our interests aligned has always been a great comfort to me and Angie. I mention that because I have had people suggest that a bad round or tournament could be the result of me being distracted by my off-course interests. The reality is the opposite. Golf has always been the thing that causes me the most stress, even when I don't show it. In my world, catching up on the comings and goings of the baseball team or the car dealership is a welcome distraction for someone like me who has a hard time sitting still and needs to keep my mind occupied.

One of the things that Quint and Sandy taught me was not to look at just your own businesses but to see the whole fabric of life that you're a part of. With every business venture I undertake, I'm learning new things about how to run a business, but also how it impacts the community. I can see work opportunities for young people growing up and full-time employment for others who are ready to set down roots and maybe start families. I suppose I could sit back and watch my money grow in some bank account, but where's the fun in that? The real benefit of gaining financial security is the opportunity to give back and help the economy and community that gave me my start.

Ultimately, I think I moved back home because I was still following my dad's advice that I should try to be a leader and not a follower; and the simple fact was that if I was going to be a leader, I wanted to live somewhere I could have a real impact. In Scottsdale or Orlando, I was an athlete who grew up somewhere else. Pensacola is where I dreamed my dreams and became who I am. Besides, Pensacola was on the move and had that special small-town pride you rarely find in a bigger city. Growing up, the town used to love it when Roy Jones Jr., the great champion boxer who grew up in Pensacola and still lives there, used to end interviews by saying, "Pensacola *in the house!*" I wanted to tap into that kind of energy.

Deep down, I suppose I didn't want to come home until I'd proved to myself that I had "made it," that I had figured out who I was. That second green jacket gave me the validation I needed. This time around, I was ready to wear it around town a little as a guest speaker at schools and youth sports events and other public events. Given that I'm a shy person by nature (despite my propensity to dance in silly social media videos), I'm more visible around Pensacola than I ever thought I would be. But I'm good with that. No, I'm better than good with that. I'm great with it if it helps make my hometown prosper.

I look at Pensacola today and see a vibrant and growing city with several colleges and a growing university, a world-class hospital, and a professional baseball team that everybody loves and that loves the city in return. I'm so proud to be playing my part in its story and I think we're just getting started. Gosh, it sounds like I'm planning on running for mayor! Just kidding. Back in 2016 I made a similar joke, only to have a reporter ask me what my priority would be if I were mayor. Without much thought I gave a fairly serious response, saying I would focus on improving our education system. Before I knew it, some people started thinking I was serious about running for mayor and it became a bit of a story locally. About a week or so later, a local newspaper ran a poll asking residents who they wanted to see run for mayor. My name wasn't just in the poll—it turned out a decent portion of the local population might have been willing to vote for me. I'm not sure if that says more about me or how people feel about career politicians, but Randall even got calls from several active politicians wanting to know if I was going to enter the race for mayor.

Hmmm . . .

CHAPTER 18

Back to the Basics—Having Fun

I opened this book with a chapter called "Rock Bottom" because I wanted to be open and honest about a very difficult time in my life. I felt that my kneeling on the floor and crying to God for some kind of guidance would not only represent exactly what happened but also lay bare a pivotal moment in my life. It was a bit of a risky way to start a book about a well-known sports figure, but part of my point was that maybe I wasn't as well-known as people thought I was. I also felt that many of you may be able to relate to the feeling that what people see on the outside isn't always an accurate reflection of what is going on inside.

Well, with this current chapter, we have come back full circle to that moment when I was on the floor. The writer Harper Lee wrote that when you're at the top, there's only one way to go. During the stretch of time from 2010 to early 2016, I was pretty close to the top no matter how I looked at it. In 2012 and 2014, I won two Masters championships. In the summer of 2015, my golf ranking reached an all-time high of second in the world, and I was winning more prize money than I had ever thought possible. I had lucrative sponsorship deals with companies like

PING, the brand of clubs I had played since childhood, and the luxury French watchmaker Richard Mille, among others. I was living at the prestigious Isleworth Golf Course near Orlando, Florida, in a big lake house that gave me the privacy I cherished so much, but I also got to travel around the world doing what I loved to do: playing golf and having fun with Angie. And I had my beautiful wife and children to provide for as our family life began to flourish.

If all this sounds like a life I should have felt blessed to live, let me assure you that I did. The problem was that I wasn't always free to live it on my own terms. That's because we lived our life in the public eye, with the result that the details of our lives often didn't seem to belong to us. As an athlete I always knew that what I did on the golf course would be heavily scrutinized, but that hasn't made it easy to accept criticism, especially when the criticism misses the mark. At the same time, being frequent vocal supporters about our adoptions had brought a spotlight on our whole family, one that perhaps burned a bit brighter than we expected. Over time, we began to realize that our role as adoption spokespersons reached beyond families that might be looking to adopt, to our kids' friends and parents, who would bring it up with our kids. Admittedly, we began to wonder if it was fair to put our kids through that at such a young age.

Angie and I also began to feel that we had to be the perfect parents, to set some unachievable level of perfection to prove we were worthy. We even had discussion about how, or even if, we should discipline our children in a restaurant for fear someone would say we were mean parents. It was as though we were living in fear of something going wrong. Perhaps it was an accumulation of past events that created this stress. For better or worse we had learned the power of the media, and social media in particular.

Be it the 2013 Travelers debacle, the General Lee controversy, the trip to France, or the 2016 Ryder Cup, we had seen things go from good to bad in the blink of an eye a few too many times.

What it comes down to is that when you achieve a certain amount of fame, you're no longer allowed to make mistakes—or even appear to have made mistakes. You are expected to live the perfect life, and none of us do. If you don't, there is no telling what stories can take hold. I still watch the Golf Channel and post things on social media, but I tune out when the news is about me. Whatever amount of pleasure I would get from any-thing positive the news might say about me pales in comparison to the degree of pain I will feel when the news is negative. The negatives throw everything out of balance and exert far greater damage than they should. I don't believe I am unique in that regard, as I suspect many of you find it hard not to overreact when negative things are said about you too.

I am sure that you have thought about such things as they pertain to your own life, but I'd like to share with you the way I dealt with the problem. The great golfing legend Bobby Jones once said that it is just as true in life as in golf that you have to learn to play your ball *where it lies*. I could keep swinging in des-peration, or I could rediscover the joy I always felt as a kid playing with Randall at Tanglewood. In his own way but in a language I understood to my core, God picked me up from the floor and told me what I needed to do: I chose to make golf and life fun again. To live the life I wanted, not the life people expected me to live.

———

The things that give me the greatest pleasure in life are being a husband and father, so rather than spend most of my time without Angie and the kids, whenever we can, Angie and I bring the kids along with us to tournaments in our RV. We started doing this in 2018 and found that some of the other players brought their families along, too, so our kids have gotten to know each other, and it creates a nice home away from home on the road. It doesn't hurt that our RV offers, shall we say, a bit more amenities than your average RV. (For those in the know, we have a Prevost.) We started with a double slide made by Florida Coach, but recently upgraded to a custom quad slide from Marathon. Most of the time we refer to it as the "bus." Having a constant "home" on tour that is the same every week has helped make life on tour a little more enjoyable. I no longer have to worry about the hotel mattress being too hard or too soft every week, and I am able to eat in rather than going out every night. It may not sound like much, but the comfort of something familiar every week has helped. The kids mainly like it because sometimes they get to cut school a little early and join me on the road for a few days. Kids, right?

In 2018, I did something that I probably would not have been able to bring myself to do in the past: I played in the NBA All-Star Celebrity Game on a Friday night, while simultaneously competing in a PGA tournament, the Genesis Open held at the Riviera Country Club. I had won the Riviera tournament twice, in 2014 and 2016. This time, it coincided with the NBA All-Star Weekend, and I was invited to be on Team Los Angeles Clippers.

In the past, I might have declined to play in the NBA event for fear of being injured and angering my sponsors who wanted to see me focus on the golf at Riviera. But I love basketball and always enjoy trash-talking with basketball players, so, in keeping with my new commitment to finding fun wherever I could, I threw caution to the wind, even joking that I would withdraw from Riviera if my tee time didn't allow me to get to the basketball game. I became Mr. Hollywood for a weekend. I met with the cast of *The Big Bang Theory*, one of my favorite shows, and visited with Ellen DeGeneres. At one point during the All-Star game, in a fit of madness, I tried to score over NBA legend Tracy McGrady, who seemed to feel that this Florida boy wasn't going to score after all. As McGrady went to block my shot, it felt like his entire body from the knees up was soaring over me, and as he swatted away the ball, I saw my life and career flash before my eyes.

And guess what? No, I didn't make the shot and enjoy a Hollywood ending. I ended up jamming my finger and injuring myself just as I'd always feared. The next day when I woke up it was quite sore, and I was worried I might not be able to hold the club well enough to play. It was as if all the voices in my head (including Angie's) were saying, "I told you so." But then something awesome happened: I went back to finish the tournament and wound up winning for the third time at Riviera with a score of 12 under par.

Somewhere along the way, I began to accept that there is a bit of a pattern that connects my life and my performance on the golf course. After we got Caleb, I won my first Masters, and it was in the midst of getting Dakota that I won the HSBC in China. In 2015, as I was rediscovering my hometown of Pensacola, I played some of the best golf of my life. There is no doubt that I play my best golf and act like the best possible version of myself off the course when I am living my life, having fun, and not worrying about every little thing.

I'm not sure why it took me so long to fully acknowledge the connection. After all, when I started my good run of play back in 2011 and 2012, I was having fun and expressing myself in new ways all the time. When I cut the first Golf Boys music video with Ben Crane, Rickie Fowler, and Hunter Mahan back in 2011, I wasn't worried about what other people would think; we were just having fun.

The seed for Golf Boys was planted when Ben filmed a one-minute video tribute for a friend of his who was celebrating his fiftieth birthday. Ben was having all sorts of trouble coming up with a concept for the tribute. Ben tells it this way: "I went out to my back porch and set up my camera on a tripod and told my friend how much our friendship meant, and after about forty seconds of this, I knew it was certifiably the most boring thing I've ever seen in my life. So, I ended up talking to this creative videographer friend about coming up with a plan B. My friend, Sam Martin, was working on a dance video for a charity and suggested I take a shot at doing a dance video. So they got me all dressed up and I wrote some catchy happy birthday lyrics and did it. After it was shown at the party—the party was full of celebrities—who else but George Clooney walked up to me and told me how much he loved the video."

When Ben showed it to us, we all said, "Man, we've got to do a dance video." At first, we wanted to call ourselves 99 Degrees—which was one better than the pop group 98 Degrees—but then realized most people wouldn't know who we were. So we chose Golf Boys and modeled ourselves off of the boy bands. We shot our first video "Oh!" in Ben's house in Dallas. We wore ridiculous outfits and got a quick dance tutorial from this guy named Andre, who Ben knew. The lyrics were written by Ben's friend Matt Carney. Then we did the video. It came out the day before the 2011 US Open. I remember people yelling lines from it to us the next day. The concept kind of died down until I won the

Masters, after which it took on a life of its own. We did another video in 2013 called "Oh, Oh!" We got something like six million hits on YouTube.

The money we've made from the videos has gone to an organization called Charity: Water, which provides drinking water for people in developing nations. I don't know for sure if we will ever make another Golf Boys video, but part of me hopes we do. Maybe we can celebrate our tenth anniversary with a new release.

Throughout 2017 and early 2018, I kept encouraging myself with the idea that life should be fun and to stop worrying about every little thing. That message was reinforced by Angie, Teddy, and Randall. Luckily, my mindset slowly improved, and I started to regain my weight. I will likely always battle those negative voices in my head. But I have learned to trust my faith and to cling to more of the positive thoughts that come to me. As I regained control of my mind, I went on to win three times on the PGA Tour in 2018. Since most people had no idea what I had been going through, many people assumed the resurgence in my game was a result of switching back to the Titleist ball, but I knew my poor play had started long before I changed balls. My best playing didn't come back until I regained control of the fear and anxieties that were clouding my mind.

CHAPTER 19

Reflections on the Ryder Cup

Golf is usually a relentlessly individual sport where success comes to those who can maintain their composure, both mentally and physically. When you succeed or fail at golf, the public light shines directly on you, and you become part of a wider public conversation. Neither of these conditions of professional golf play particularly well to my personality, which is intensely private and highly strung. But there's another side to being a golfer that involves being part of a team, and what I've discovered is that this side brings out an entirely different part of me.

Following the European victory in the 2014 Ryder Cup, the PGA of America set up a task force to help figure out a way for the United States to compete more successfully in the Cup. The US had lost three consecutive Ryder Cups and eight of the last ten competitions, which took place every year at alternating US and European locations. The task force looked at several issues, including the selection of the Ryder Cup captain and vice-captains and the team selection process. The task force consisted of three PGA officials and eight players with Ryder Cup experience, including three previous Ryder Cup captains, Raymond

Floyd, Tom Lehman, and Davis Love III. Working to create the best opportunity for a US victory, the task force tapped veterans like Rickie Fowler, Jim Furyk, Phil Mickelson, Steve Stricker, and Tiger Woods.

Together, they decided that Davis would be the best captain.

I had competed in the 2014 Cup and was eager to make the team again in 2016 and, I hoped, help the US turn things around. Nothing would be sweeter for me than to be on the team that regained the Cup for the first time since 1989.

So you can imagine my disappointment when I wasn't chosen that year. In 2016, the newly retooled and reorganized Ryder Cup team decided to go in a different direction despite my having won that year, accumulating the ninth highest Ryder Cup points total and being ranked seventh in the world. It's likely that no player with the equivalent performance during his prime had been passed up as a captain's pick since the European team first employed wild-card choices in 1979. The media were bound to have a field day.

Which they did.

The buzz was that all those associated with the selection process thought my personality might become an issue in the team room. This would explain, so the rumors went, why Ryan Moore, J.B. Holmes, Rickie Fowler, and Matt Kuchar were chosen as the captain's picks ahead of me. Davis assured everyone that his choices had everything to do with pairing up the guys who had the best possible chance of winning and nothing to do with personalities.

I believe what he told the press was true because he told me the same thing. It was always about putting the right people together on the golf course. We didn't just need a big hitter or putter, said Davis, we needed strokes gained with every club.

Everybody on the team was at the top of the Tour in wedge play, which I was not. It was just simple statistics and the belief that a different type of player provided the team the best chance to win. If they had been looking for a big hitter or a pure ball striker, I probably would have been a first pick.

I was hurt and baffled by the decision. But after my initial disappointment, I had an epiphany: rather than pout, I told myself, I would try to use the Ryder Cup as an opportunity to show the world who I *really* was. I respected the heck out of Davis and refused to allow any bitterness to define our relationship or my relationship with other golfers—or to the sport I love. A lot of people didn't know who I was. They didn't know that I was a man of faith and loved representing my country. They also didn't know something else: that I loved opportunities to be of service to other people, including other golfers, because doing so would allow me to feel part of something bigger than myself.

When Davis delivered the message that I wouldn't be playing, my next conversation was with Angie. How should I react? What should I say? I looked at Angie and simply asked: "What would Jesus do?" The answer was simple. He would set all ego aside and serve others. I sensed she was hesitant, but she agreed I should offer.

So I called Davis and told him I still wanted to be a part of this team if he would have me. I told him I would be there to serve the twelve guys any way I could, whether it was helping them get a point, get a trophy, fetch them more golf balls or water bottles, or carry their bags to their car.

"I will do whatever is needed, and for me, it would be the thrill of a lifetime to be a part of this team," I said.

My offer floored Davis, and when he told the team members and assistant captains, they, too, were deeply moved. That day, Davis named me vice-captain, the final spot on the 2016 Ryder Cup team. More than just a couple of players on that team admitted they doubted they would ever be able to make the same decision I did. When I got to the practice facility where the team gathered, everybody showed great support. Besides, I was in some pretty good company. The other vice-captains were Tom Lehman, Jim Furyk, Steve Stricker, and Tiger Woods.

I knew this wasn't any kind of honorary position. I'd be dressing differently than the players, and instead of a bag of clubs I'd have a two-way radio and be responsible for doing basically whatever Davis asked me to do. Ironically, the first player who showed up for me to help was . . . Ryan Moore. I was there at the front door when he and his wife arrived at the hotel and helped carry their luggage up to their room and walked Ryan through the schedule.

Monday afternoon, after I arrived in Minnesota, I went to Davis and offered one more pair of hands. "Would you consider letting Teddy come and help the caddies?" I asked, fully aware that it wasn't common that vice-captains brought their caddies along. Davis asked a few others and agreed Teddy would be a perfect addition. I got to call Teddy, who immediately flew north. He, too, wanted to be part of this, no matter the role.

On the first morning before the tournament, we were scheduled to play a practice round and I woke up early to wait for everybody as they came down the stairs to give them instructions about what to do. The only person who Davis hadn't directly called about my role on the team was Tiger. When I met him in the lobby and started telling him what the schedule would be, he gave me a funny look and made a beeline over to ask Davis what gives.

Davis told me the story: "I told Tiger that the first thing out of Bubba's mouth when I told him he didn't make the team was, 'Okay, can I be an assistant captain?' Tiger's mouth fell open and he said 'What? That's the most unbelievable thing I've ever heard.'" It made an impression on every member of that team because I think they had all assumed I would be royally ticked off, dejected, and embarrassed by not being picked to be a player on the team.

At the beginning of the Ryder Cup tournament, which was held at the Hazeltine National Golf Club in Chaska, Minnesota, we had a big team meeting. One by one, guys got up to talk about different things. Some talked about logistics or housekeeping for the team; others gave pep talks and that sort of thing. I had this idea that came to me at some point early on. The guys were always joshing me about the fact that I don't drink. I don't just *not* drink. I have never had an alcoholic drink in my life. It just never had any appeal to me, especially the idea of waking up hungover and groggy when all I wanted to do in life was get out there on the course when the sun came up. I never understood why anybody wanted to do that to themselves.

Well, in golf, as in other sports, a lot of guys love to have a drink when the time is right. Everybody in my family drank. I think my father never missed a day in his adult life when he didn't have a drink.

Anyway, at the Ryder Cup, I raised my hand to talk and stood up on a chair. I said to the guys, "Y'all know I'm not known for drinking, but if y'all win this thing, I'll drink a beer with you!" That brought a round of laughs and guffaws, but I was serious.

Five days before the tournament began, Arnold Palmer died at the age of eighty-seven while awaiting heart surgery. Davis dedicated the match to Arnie and his golf bag was placed on the first tee during Friday's opening foursomes in honor of the great man and one of golf's most beloved figures. Team USA responded to the emotional charge by sweeping Friday's session 4–0 for the first time since 1975, which also, fittingly, was the last time Arnie led the Americans at the Ryder Cup.

The US never relinquished our lead during the tournament, and our victory was sweeter than any wine I could drink. Not only that, everything about this Cup confirmed the wisdom of Davis's picks. In 2016, each member of the US team—Matt Kuchar, Dustin Johnson, Brandt Snedeker, Ryan Moore, Brooks Koepka, Zach Johnson, J. B. Holmes, Jordan Spieth, Phil Mickelson, Jimmy Walker, Patrick Reed, and Rickie Fowler—won at least one match over the course of the week, which was also a first since 1975. Holmes, Fowler, Kuchar, and Moore, the last guy picked by Davis over me, went 7–6–0 for the week, setting a record for the most points earned by US captain's picks in a single Ryder Cup.

On Saturday night the team gathered for an intimate dinner to prepare ourselves for Sunday's round. A number of people stood to say a few words. When the room quieted down, I told everybody how honored I felt to be with them and share in what I believed would be our hard-fought victory. I'd done a little research on the topic and went on to talk about the Bible a little bit: how Jesus had twelve disciples, and how we had twelve golfers who played on the team. "Being here with you guys is probably the closest I will ever get to Jesus," I told them. "And the last couple of days were a dream come true for me and without a doubt the greatest thing I have ever experienced in golf. I am so happy for this team. This team is amazing. You embraced me with open arms."

During the Final on Sunday, that special experience became even greater. One of the ways Davis implemented his goal of "getting the right people on the golf course" involved pairing captains and assistants with players who wanted an encouraging and experienced voice beside them. Tiger went with Patrick Reed, Davis went with Jordan Spieth, and I went with Brandt Snedeker, who told Davis he wasn't going to play any singles matches without me walking "side-by-side" with him down the fairway.

And that's exactly what I did on Sunday. I started the day switching back and forth between Brandt and Ryan Moore. Then, I think it was on the third or fourth hole, I was watching Brandt play when he birdied the hole. As we prepared to begin the walk to the next hole, which was around 150 yards away, Brandt looked at me and said, "Don't even think about leaving me now. I just made a birdie." I knew exactly where Brandt was mentally. We golfers are like pitchers, a bunch of serious head cases and very superstitious. So I stayed with Brandt and stood back a little while he played, and whispered into my walkie-talkie to Teddy, who was one hole ahead of us where Ryan was playing.

"Can you go as fast as you can and get Ryan's family and bring them inside the ropes?" I said to Teddy. "Ryan is a big family man and seeing his wife and parents there being taken care of will just light him up!"

While Teddy ran off to find Ryan's family, I stayed with Brandt who was starting his move, and we really began to taste those two points. I don't recall much more about the rest of the match, but I do remember this: both Brandt and Ryan went on to win their matches, with Ryan sealing it for the US. And I remember spotting Davis at the eighteenth hole after Ryan won, where everybody was jumping up and down and cheering. I walked over to him and . . . three guesses . . . I put my head on his shoulder and sobbed my heart out. Sure, I was happy for the win, but I was happier about being with my brothers.

I didn't let go of Davis for a long time.

At some point, after the matches ended and the trophy presentation was made, everybody gathered in the team room and began offering cheers and making little speeches. I saw Brandt Snedeker pouring a bottle of beer into a Styrofoam coffee cup and heading over in my direction. He was smiling but also looked a little bit concerned. When he reached me, he whispered, "You know, Bubba, you don't have to do this . . . I'll be watching you just in case." He was probably worried I'd fall off the chair and hurt myself or become a raging alcoholic after drinking a beer! I said, "Dude, it's one beer!" I assured him my willpower was up to the task of drinking a single beer, and I drained it in one gulp while everybody cheered and laughed and drank their beers. I have to say: I didn't like the beer, but victory tasted good!

When I asked Davis to appoint me assistant captain, I never thought that I was making any kind of huge sacrifice or eating humble pie. The truth was, I just wanted so much to be a part of the team. But it turned out that a lot of players ended up seeing my appointment in this light—as taking one for the team. This misperception was actually a good thing for everybody. After 2014, when PGA America took a good look at itself, it realized that the US didn't need better golfers, it needed better teamwork and strategy. The organization saw that we may have had many of the world's best individual players but that the Europeans played better as a team. My willingness to put heart and soul into the assistant job reinforced the idea that we had to work hard to form a true team identity rather than settle for being just a collection of star individuals. People would look at me running around with a two-way radio and say, "Holy crap! That's the number-seven player in the world!"

That year I was in the process of making a concerted effort to open up, share more of me than I had been previously comfortable sharing, and, hopefully, change my image with the general public. In the spring before the Ryder Cup, I even did an interview with *60 Minutes* in which I talked about my fears of crowds and of flying. I told them I have panic attacks that are so bad I think I'm having a heart attack. Making shots and putts are easy, I said. It's the mental part of the game where I tend to fall down. But I was working on it like my life depended on becoming a better person, which was true. With help from Jesus Christ and from my family and closest friends, I knew I could progress and become a better person just as surely as I'd known I would become a better golfer back in my younger days.

I was determined to take it upon myself to tell the world who the real Bubba Watson was, but it helped a lot when guys like Brandt also went out of their way to challenge the narrative of big, bad Bubba. "I don't know where everybody gets this idea that Bubba Watson is a bad teammate. He is probably one of the best teammates you could possibly have," Brandt told one reporter. "I want that out there for everybody to hear. Bubba Watson is a great teammate. He's the most positive, self-deprecating, greatest teammate to have in the team room—100 percent behind you all the time. Great cheerleader. A guy that anybody on the team would love to play with."

Before the Cup, Brandt had told Davis that if he and I were picked for the Cup, he wanted to be my partner.

———

Back in the team room after the big win, some guys were crying, and others were hugging each other. It mattered to me a lot that, one after another, the players mentioned me in their remarks, telling the team they were honored to call me their friend and have me there as part of the team. Brandt told everybody that I was the reason he was able to "get around out there" when he beat Andy Sullivan three and one. I had been in Brandt's ear all day, walking with him every step of the way and giving him every ounce of support I had. Now he was saying, "A guy like Bubba, putting his ego to the side and saying, 'I want to be a part of this.' You need somebody like that in your corner all the time."

Davis told me that if they'd had a most valuable captain award, it would probably be mine.

I wish I could say that after the 2016 Ryder Cup I never stressed out again and never let my emotions get the better of me on the golf course. I wish I could say I've never complained to an official about a rule, lost my cool with a fan who was snapping pictures of me while I was addressing a ball, or let slip to a reporter that I wasn't crazy about the conditions of a golf course where I'd just stunk the place up. But none of it is true.

Still, I'm getting better with time. And, crazy as it sounds, I think that the struggles I've had with the mental side of my game have made me a better coach and, dare I say, captain. Empathy is an essential ingredient to successful coaching. Davis showed it by welcoming me into the team, and it's something I very much hope to continue paying forward in the years to come.

CHAPTER 20

What's Next?

I hope you have enjoyed reading about some of my ups and downs. As I said at the outset, I never wanted this book to be a tell-all or a way to get back at people or some overly commercialized product designed to please a fancy publisher either. (If I had written this years ago, the publisher probably would have required me to use Tiger's name a hundred more times and go deeper than I wanted to on my relationship with Justin Bieber.) Instead, my hope is that you have seen this as a narrative of a person who is constantly changing, striving to be better while never losing sight of who they are in a world full of challenges. If any of my challenges resonate with you or someone you know, then I hope you will find inspiration in my story. When I take my Tour card out of my wallet and put it behind glass or toss it in my keepsake drawer, I will still be me, and life will go on. The ups and downs may not be as visible, but they will still be there. The good news is that I now know more than ever, it's okay to not be okay. When I feel down, I know things will get better. I just have to stay true to myself.

The chapters in this book are built on key moments that led

to pivots in my life. If I hadn't shot 62, I might not have chosen golf over baseball. If I turned pro early and skipped college, I would not have met Angie. If Angie and I didn't have a strong relationship built on our shared faith, I might not have been able to survive in the public eye. Those pivots have brought me to this final chapter and the realization that this book itself can be seen as a pivot to the next chapter of my life.

And what will that be? When I was a kid, I dreamed of playing professional golf. As a professional golfer, I dreamed of making the PGA Tour. As a PGA Tour member, I dreamed of winning my first tournament. I never thought I would get more than one tournament win, and now I am up to thirteen world-wide with an amazing *two* majors. I could set my clubs aside tomorrow and not be disappointed in what I have accomplished. But I am not ready to sign my last scorecard yet. The history of golf tells us it is tough for a golfer to be ultra-competitive into his late forties. But at the same time, I have contemporaries like Phil Mickelson who have not only stayed competitive but even won the PGA Championship, a major, after turning fifty. So I know it can be done. The guys who have had long careers have often had long, flexible swings and hit the ball longer than most. I fit into that mold.

Most of this book was written during the COVID-19 pandemic. I actually thought that given my unease around large crowds, I would welcome the lack of fans at tournaments brought on by the pandemic. Well, after playing without the fans for the better part of a year, I have to say that I miss them quite a lot. I miss their energy, their warmth, and their support. I miss their love. But even more than this, if I'm being totally honest, I have grown to enjoy being in the public eye. I no longer have fantasies of disappearing from public life. To the contrary,

I figure I'll always be a public figure to some degree, whether I am playing golf, serving as a spokesperson for adoption or some other concern, or working to make a difference in my community.

I have made no secret of my desire to be inducted into the World Golf Hall of Fame and my dream of one day being selected as US Ryder Cup captain. I view both as similar kinds of levels of achievement that signify a golfer's standing at the pinnacle of the game. While there is no specific formula for getting into the Hall of Fame, I am only a few wins away from what I see as "qualifying" for the Hall. If I can get to fifteen PGA Tour wins or three majors, I hope I would have a good chance of being selected.

As I get older, I have devoted myself to getting a little better each day in just about every imaginable way. Shoot, I have even tried to learn how to breathe better. Yeah, you heard that right. The guy who used to insist on doing almost everything alone hired someone to help work on breathing. I will not divulge all my secrets here, but the goal is to improve my ability to handle stress and anxiety, both on and off the golf course.

Back in 2018, some friends told me about the impact of CBD on anxiety and stress, so I reached out to my doctor for advice, and I started taking CBD twice daily, once when I wake up in the morning and once again before I go to sleep. It is a little drop that I place under my tongue. At first a lot of people seemed to think I was crazy, saying CBD was going to make me test positive for marijuana and get in trouble with the PGA Tour. They thought this because CBD comes from the same plant as marijuana; however, the products I take do not contain detectable THC (THC is the psychoactive element in cannabis—the stuff that gets you high). To be sure, I have performed my own drug test to be safe and ensure I did not accidently test positive for anything banned by the Tour. It shouldn't have been necessary, but can you imagine what the media would do with that one?

———————

After the 2012 Masters, I used to tell people I was planning my life so that I didn't have to play golf after forty. As a result, a lot of people thought my goal was to play until I was forty and then retire. A few of my sponsors even began to ask if I was serious about retiring at forty. I understand why people thought that, but I never really planned to walk away. My financial goals weren't about quitting the game; in fact, it was the opposite. I wanted to be in a position to play for the love of the game and not chase the money, because I knew that I played my best golf when I was out there playing for fun. Except for a couple of bad spells when I let the pressure to perform get to me in 2013 and again in late 2016 and into 2017, at the expense of my mental health and behavior, I think I did a good job of following my plan. I can truly say that today I am playing for the love of the game, a love that I will always have. If I were to retire, I would probably just play more golf, so what's the point in retiring?

I have been lucky to have close friends around me to help me work toward becoming a better person. People like Angie, Teddy, Randall, the team at PROSPORT Management, and many others. Without them my life and career could have turned out very differently. I think I have the ability to help many younger players in the game as a mentor or maybe even as an agent or manager for other players. Having been in their shoes, I recognize that many of them need similar kinds of support in their lives. But I also have come to realize that many of them are not as fortunate as

I've been in having a loving, supportive team around to help me weather the ups and downs of a life in golf.

I understand a player's need to find ways to escape from the stress of sports. I've tried all sorts of things, from buying cars, to playing video games, to Bible study. But some players are tempted into more destructive ways of finding their "nothing places." You don't have to follow golf too closely to see the rumors about players who have gone to Las Vegas and lost a whole lot of money. Players also hurt themselves by allowing the media to tell their stories for them. As I have learned, sharing yourself with the media involves a delicate balance of openness and privacy, but if you don't open up to some degree and let people see behind the curtain, the media will happily fill the void for better or worse.

Not every golfer is willing to put themselves out there on social media like I have done, and even if they did, there would be no guarantee that "getting themselves out there" would turn out well for them. But my experience says that it can be good for people to figure out who they are and find their voice. In my case, I have always felt that being good at golf was part of God's plan for me, and that as a man of faith I have an obligation to use the platform golf has provided me to the best of my ability.

———

When I am home in Pensacola, I like to help coach Caleb's and Dakota's sports teams. Once, we were playing a makeup baseball game that had been rained out, and the umpire did not show up. I told everybody I would do it and went and stood behind second base since I did not have a protective vest. I think I was pretty impartial, but it is hard watching the game and keeping the pitch count.

I like being able to combine golf with my other interests. Every year I play in the Zurich Classic in New Orleans, which is a three- or four-hour trip from Pensacola by bus. For several years running, a group of seventy-five or so Blue Wahoos season-ticket holders, sponsors, and front office staff have traveled over on two charter buses to watch me play in the Zurich Classic. It may not seem like much, but I love hearing stories from people who have gone on those trips that have never been to a PGA Tour tournament before.

In December of 2020, I played in the 2020 PNC Championship, formerly known as the Father/Son Challenge, with Angie's dad, Wayne Ball, who I call "Baller." The event has loosened up its requirements so players can team up with daughters, fathers, grandsons, and in-laws. Caleb made the trip as well. Maybe he was scouting the competition for when he will be old enough to play in the tournament. Tiger and his son, Charlie, and John Daly and his son, David, were also there. It was a wonderful family-oriented experience I would love to be able to share with Caleb and Dakota one day.

I still play golf and explore business opportunities with my childhood friend Randall Wells. We plan to continue on with business pursuits that have meaning to us and are fun. We aren't out to make a fortune as much as we are looking to make a difference. I have always been very selective about the companies I work with, but I am perhaps even more selective today. Any time I serve as an ambassador or spokesperson, I want to know that I can truly trust the brand. While owning a piece of the companies I work with is not always possible, it is something I often explore. It is that whole leadership orientation I absorbed early on from my dad, right? My latest venture is that I became part owner of a lifestyle clothing brand called Linksoul, which is a small entrepreneurial company founded by John Ashworth and Geoff Cunningham. I always loved John Ashworth's clothes growing up and am excited to be working with him from an ownership position because it combines three of my passions: golf, clothing, and entrepreneurship.

I love the process of getting ourselves aligned with a company so that if they do well, I do well, and if I do well, they do well. I care about whether or not they make a profit, not just whether or not they pay me for my name. Part of what drew me to Linksoul is the company's philosophy. The idea behind Linksoul is that it is about more than clothes: it is the collective life work of people who care about each other and enjoy collaborating. "More than golf" is one of their mottos, as is *Tempus Fugit*, which is a Latin phrase that loosely translates to "time flies." As I got to know the team at Linksoul, I couldn't help but feel like we were all traveling the same road, knowing that life is bigger than what we do day-to-day.

My relationship with PING is an exception because it is family-owned and it was not realistic to seek ownership. Still, I wanted a permanent partnership with them that recognized our lifelong relationship. When I started with PING they were known for putters and irons. Drivers weren't really their thing; but today, I believe they truly make the best drivers available in the market. It has been a lot of fun trying to influence their product line over the years, be it the actual club design or something as mundane as the paint scheme. Here is a funny example: For the past seven or eight years, their drivers have had a black matte finish. Before this, I think PING tended to make glossy painted drivers—the kind that would catch a glint off the sun and maybe distract a player during a shot. At the time I had a custom Mercedes G63 Wagon, which happened to be painted matte black, that I drove to PING.

"This is what color the club should be," I told them as we stood in the parking lot of PING headquarters. Now I don't know that they changed the color because of that one day, but I like to think I helped push them along. So if somebody says PING is the Mercedes of golf clubs, you'll know why!

At the end of 2020, I signed a lifetime contract with PING, which means I'll represent the manufacturer well beyond my PGA Tour–playing career. I consider the company's owner, John Solheim, to be a true friend and mentor of mine. In some ways he has been like a father figure for me over the years, and I can't thank the Solheim family enough for their support during my career. The kind of longevity we have shared is rare in our industry, as is the number of years—I think we are heading into thirteen now—that Teddy and I have worked together as a player and caddie.

On top of loving a business and having fun with it, I also enjoy being involved with businesses that deepen my connection to the community. That means doubling down to make sure Bubba's Sweet Spot continues to provide a safe, friendly place for kids and adults to visit in downtown. It means carrying on Sandy Sansing's good work not only in the car business but also in the community by sponsoring youth sports teams and tournaments, to give kids a chance to reach for the sky in their chosen sport. It means helping to give downtown Pensacola a strong anchor by having its own baseball team in the Blue Wahoos. Downtowns feed the larger community by offering a location where people from all walks of life can meet, take in a ball game, and share, oh, I don't know, an ice cream cone.

I hope that you feel you know me a little better now—that you know where I come from, how faith has played a role in my life, and what I'm trying to do with my life. When I started working on this book with my coauthor, Don Yaeger, I somewhat jokingly told Don that I don't really like to read books. Having gone through this experience, I have a much greater appreciation for anyone who has ever written a book. I also feel like I know myself better.

That's kind of the point of opening up and writing a book like this, isn't it? Life, like golf, is filled with ups and downs. To win, you have to manage both.

ACKNOWLEDGMENTS

I would like to thank my coauthor, Don Yaeger, for guiding me through the process of writing this book. Without his patience and persistence, this book may never have seen the light of day. Don first approached me about writing a book together several years back, unaware of the personal struggles and severe anxiety I was experiencing at the time. He waited patiently for several years, without knowing if I would ever be ready to tell the world about my journey. I doubt he had any idea what he was getting himself into when he reached out that first time. Don also connected me with Dave Moore, who helped edit the manuscript, along with the team at W Publishing—including Damon Reiss, Stephanie Newton, Dawn Holloman, Carrie Marrs, and Kyle Olund. I am especially grateful to Kyle for all his editorial support and for believing in this project, and to Caren Wolfe, Allison Carter, and Alex Woods from W's marketing team for tirelessly promoting *Up and Down*. Bringing this book to life and getting it into your hands was truly a team effort.

I would also like to thank everyone who graciously gave their time and knowledge to this project, including but not limited to my wife, Angie Watson; my mom, Molly Watson; Teddy Scott;

Captain Davis Love III; Brandt Snedeker; Ben Crane; Webb Simpson; Quint Studer; Sandy Sansing; Coach Chris Haack; Randall Wells; Jens Beck; Kimber Fierro; and my entire team at PROSPORT Management.

None of this would have been possible without people who have supported and believed in me throughout my life, be it on the golf course, during the adoption of our two children, or in developing my faith. I have lived a blessed life, and the number of people who have impacted me is too many to mention, but if you are one of them, I hope you know that I appreciate and love you.

Last but not least, I would like to thank Mom and Dad for giving me the foundation to become the person I am today.

ABOUT THE AUTHOR

Growing up in the small town of Bagdad outside of Pensacola, Florida, Bubba Watson dreamed of being a champion golfer. He has more than fulfilled that dream with twelve wins on the PGA Tour, including two Masters—and he did so while smashing drives with a hot pink driver.

Success on golf's biggest stage made Bubba Watson famous, but he has always been more than a golfer in the eyes of those closest to him. A lively debater who loves to question the status quo, Bubba is always looking for a way to make a positive impact on the world. The idea of becoming an author, however, never crossed his mind until he found the strength to begin talking to those closest to him about his personal struggles.

Once he began to open up about his experience with anxiety, the desire to be a better husband and friend, and the difficulty of balancing his professional and personal life, he quickly realized that the very things he thought made him unique were actually the things that made him just like everyone else. It was at that moment he knew that others could benefit from hearing his story.

Away from the course, Bubba is an adventurous goofball who often entertains his fans with silly videos on social media. But it's his life away from the public eye that truly defines him. A man of faith, he loves spending time with his wife, Angie, their two children, Caleb and Dakota, and his friends. Bubba is also a big supporter of his hometown, where he is part owner of the AA Pensacola Blue Wahoos baseball team, a car dealership, a candy store, and a driving range. His family's commitment to their community and the opportunity to help improve others' lives, however, provide him the greatest satisfaction.